The Fal[illegible]e Causewa[illegible] Coast

1939-1945

BUSHMILLS

Compiled and Edited by
GLENDA RODGERS

Published by Glenda Rodgers
49 Huey Crescent, Bushmills,
Co. Antrim, N. Ireland, BT57 8QZ
email: glendarodgers@btinternet.com

July 2008

ISBN 978-0-9559510-0-8

Compiled and edited by Glenda Rodgers

Cover painting by Gerard Law

Printed by
Coleraine Printing Company
117 Ballycastle Road, Coleraine BT52 2DZ
Telephone: (028) 7035 4873

BUSHMILLS

1939-1945

Taukkyan Cemetery, Burma 2008

"We shall fight on the beaches, we shall fight on the landing grounds, we shall fight in the fields and in the streets, we shall fight in the hills; we shall never surrender"

Introduction

While researching this book, many people have asked me how I became interested in World War Two. When I was quite young I would often visit my great grandmother, Katie Mc Allister. She would take out an old box tied up with a red ribbon, and proceed to show me the contents.

In here she kept all her treasured memories, and each time she would take out battered old photographs and much read over letters and explain to me that were sent to her, by her only son Jim, who had been killed in action, while serving in the Royal Navy during the second world war.

My father James Rodgers who himself served in the Royal Navy during the fifties, also told me of his cousin, Robert Glenn, who as a Chief Petty Officer lost his life, while serving on probably the most well known of ships in world war two, namely H.M.S. Hood. There were pictures and artefacts belonging to both these sailors at home and that is what started my interest.

In1989 I visited the Ulster Tower at the Somme, in France with my father, and Robert Thompson. Being there on the 1st July and visiting the war graves of the men from Bushmills who died in the Great War, was a very moving experience for us. Over the next few years I returned to the Somme with Robert, and we spent a week at a time finding and visiting the last resting places of our men from Bushmills. During one of these trips I got the idea of doing something similar to Robert, for the men of the second world war.

After taking the names from the war memorial, I started my research by getting in contact with the Commonwealth War Graves Commission. At first slowly by letter and then later by Internet. Through their efforts I was able to find out exactly where each service man was buried. Many hours were spent in the library going over the old newspapers of that period in time.

The first war grave that I visited, outside Bushmills was that of Charles Joseph Atkinson, who is buried in Abbeville at the Somme and the last, was that of James Andrew McCaughan who lies with his fallen comrades in Rangoon Cemetery, Burma.

At one time I thought that it was sad that so many men were buried away from home, so far away that their families could not visit on a regular basis. I have since changed my mind, as they are beside their comrades, the cemeteries are all beautiful, whether there are a few men buried there, or a thousand, so peaceful and immaculately kept. Open to the public at all times and always visited.

During this research I have met lots of people and made many friends, I have been lucky to have been able to visit all the burial places of the men from our town of Bushmills who gave their lives for us. I would like to take this opportunity to thank Danny McCormick and John Elliott for the opportunity to go to Norway for the anniversary of James Elliott's death in Sondeled and also Joan and Mike Sharpe for a great World War Two trip to Burma.

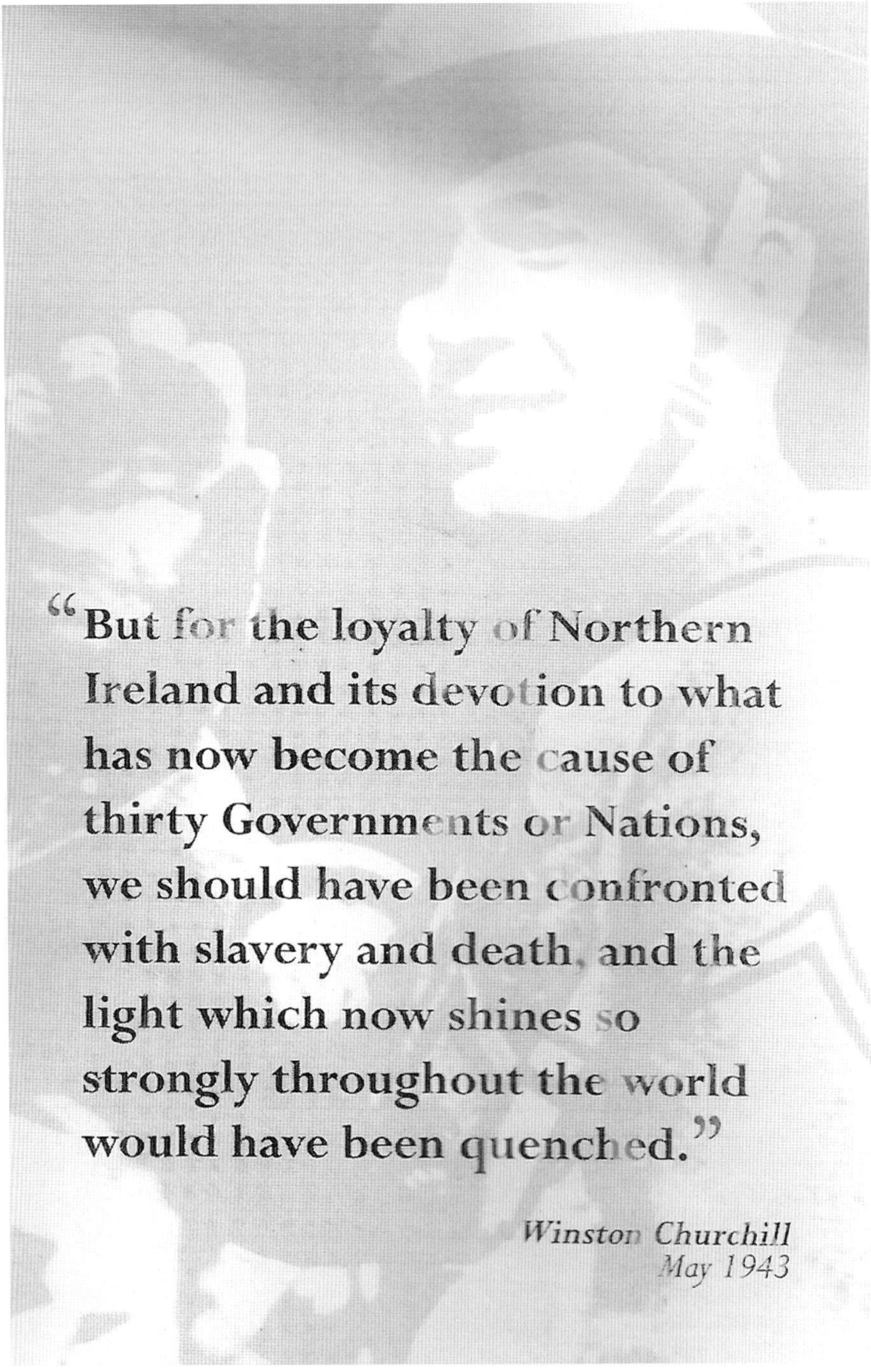

"But for the loyalty of Northern Ireland and its devotion to what has now become the cause of thirty Governments or Nations, we should have been confronted with slavery and death, and the light which now shines so strongly throughout the world would have been quenched."

Winston Churchill
May 1943

Thanks

ROBERT THOMPSON

Robert has published many books on the Great War, and his help, advice and encouragement is much appreciated.

NICK FEAR

Nick is a professional researcher, who spent a lot of his time at Kew in London, looking up service records and army diaries of the men from Bushmills.

IAN ALEXANDER

Ian Alexander from the War Research Society in Birmingham. No war grave anywhere in the world was out of the way for him and his crew, on any of his Battlefield Tours that I needed to visit.

VINCE COOKE

Vince served with the South Staffordshire Regiment, and was based in Northern Ireland during his National Service. I met him in Normandy on the 59th Anniversary of D.Day and we have covered most of the north of France together.

FAMILIES

To compile all this information together would not have been possible without help from the families of the men from our town who gave their lives in WW2.

I would especially like to thank, Matt Clyde, Mrs Lily Montgomery, Dan and Willie Hanna, Mrs Joan Graham, Mrs Sadie Sinclair, Ann Cochrane, Mrs Margaret Thompson, Joan Glenn, William McLearnon and his mother Kitty McLearnon,.Mrs Annie Freeman, Mrs Maggie Patton, Mrs Murial Meyler, James Rodgers, James Watters, Dan Cochrane, Dan Morton, Mrs Tilly Elliott of Turfahun, Susan Valantine, Noel and Joyce Rankin, Mrs Nellie Elliott of Ballytober, Frank Scott, John Elliott, John and Nan Moore, Mrs Dorothy Verner, Mr Billy McCollum and Jackie Kerr.

I would also like to thank Mrs Edith Thompson, David Speers, Mrs A. Bustard, Margorie Geary, Jim Meadows, Keith Beattie and Karen Smith of Coleraine Printing Company.

KILLED IN THE 1939–1945 WAR
SUB LIEUT JAMES W McMULLAN BUSHMILLS R N
C P OFFICER JAMES McALISTER BALLINASTRAID R N
" " WILLIAM SMITH " " R N
" " ROBERT GLENN " R N
A B ROBERT QUIGG ARABOY R N
" ALLAN LAMONT BUSHMILLS R N
" SAMUEL MORTON BALLYTOBER R N
SERGEANT WALTER G ASCOUGH BUSHMILLS R I G
" " DAVID ESDALE " " R S F
" " JOHN McGAUGHEY TURFAHUN R I F
" " HENRY ELLIOTT " " R I F
CORPORAL FRED WILKINSON BUSHMILLS R I F
PRIVATE ANDREW McCAUGHAN " CAMERONS
" " SAMUEL McKEAGUE " R P C
" " WILLIAM J TWEED " " R I F
" " CHARLES J ATKINSON LISSENDUFF R S R
" " WILLIAM COCHRANE DUNDERAVE R A
" " THOMAS HANNA BALLYHENLIN R U R
" " ROBERT MAXWELL BUSHFOOT R A S C
" " ALBERT MORTON BALLYTOBER R I R
" " JOSEPH WATTERS BUSHMILLS R U R
" " DAVID SMILEY " CAMERONS
SERGEANT WILLIAM CLYDE STRANALANE R A F
" " JAMES ELLIOTT TURFAHUN R A F
" " JAMES McCREADY BALLYCLOUGH R A F
" " WILLIAM J RANKIN " " R A F
GUNNER WILLIAM KERR LISNAGUNAGH R A
L A C W VIOLET F MOORE PORTBALLINTRAE WAAF
2nd OFFICER FRANCIS CALLAGHAN BUSHMILLS M N
O S JAMES SINCLAIR WHITE PARK M N
DIED FROM EFFECTS OF 1939–1945 WAR
PRIVATE SAMUEL MAXWELL BUSHFOOT R P C
" " SAMUEL ALEXANDER BUSHMILLS R A
" " WILLIAM WATT " " R P C

Roll of Honour

JUST AS THE SUN WENT DOWN

After the din of the battles roar
Just at the close of the day,
Wounded and bleeding upon the field
Two dying soldiers lay.

One held a ringlet of thin grey hair
One held a lock of brown,
Bidding each other a last farewell
Just as the sun went down.

One thought of Mother at home
Feeble and old and grey,
One of a sweetheart in town
Happy young and gay.

One kissed the ringlet of thin grey hair
One kissed the lock of brown,
Bidding farewell to the stars and stripes
Just as the sun went down.

One knew the joys of a Mothers love
One of a sweetheart fair,
Thinking of home they laid side by side
Breathing a farewell prayer.

One for his Mother so old and grey
One for his love in town,
They closed their eyes to the earth and skies
Just as the sun went down.

Then came the news from a comrades lips
One who had survived the fight,
Sweetheart and Mother sat listening there
Oh what a pitiful sight.

Two hearts nigh broken, two noble lives lost
Fighting defending the Crown,
Still they were proud of the heroes who died
Just as the sun went down.

Maggie Hemphill Ballylough, Bushmills
24th May, 1942

Charles Joseph Atkinson

Private 5727920

7th Bn., Royal Sussex Regiment

Died Tuesday, 21st May 1940.

Age 32

Charles Joseph Atkinson was the son of Lt. Col. Francis Salisbury Atkinson and Violet Agnes Atkinson of Ballaghmore, Portballintrae, and brother of Denis.

Lt. Col. Francis S. Atkinson served with the Inniskilling Dragoons and the Royal Army Service Corps, both he and his son Denis are buried in St. Colmans Parish churchyard, Dervock.

DIED ON ACTIVE SERVICE

ATKINSON- Private Charles Joseph, elder son of the late Colonel F.S. Atkinson, of Lissanduff, Portballintrae,serving with the Royal Sussex Regiment, was killed in action between may, 1940 and June 9, 1940

Deeply regretted

Charles Atkinson is commemorated in Dunluce Parish Church

In the second week of May, 1940, The German Army Group "A" broke through at Sedan in the Ardennes in their advance to the Channel Ports. To meet this threat the order was given to the G.H.Q. reserve troops of the B.E.F. to proceed to Abbeville.

This order affected Charles Joseph Atkinson's Battalion.

ACTION OF THE 7th BATTALION THE ROYAL SUSSEX REGIMENT B.E.F. MAY, 1940.

On the 19th May 1940, the Battalion was watching the destruction of Amiens by dive bombers nearly all day. Hundreds of troops were evacuating the area, and only the 7th Battalion and a few Royal Engineers were left. Amiens was bombed all night without a break, fires were started, a petrol dump nearby was set alight and the Germans were only 30 kilometres away.

The next day Amiens was to suffer even more bombardment, the 7th Battalion remained in its position. At about 13.30 hours as the soldiers were having a meal of bully beef and stew, they heard the sound of artillery fire, the men were told that it was the French soldiers having artillery practice.

In fact the Battalion was being attacked by enemy infantry in small groups, under the cover of mortar bombs and shell-fire.

The C.O. gave orders to fix bayonets and charge, smoke bombs were fired and the men got over a bank.

They moved across a ploughed field, and there they were confronted by German tanks which opened fire and caused numerous casualties.

At this time Abbeville was in flames, the survivors of the Battalion moved at once and crawled through a corn field for a quarter of a mile. After waiting in a wood until darkness fell, they made their way back to Rouen.

Four men from the mortars had no map or compass and took seven days to walk the whole way to the camp. The French peasants were generous and helpful, but were afraid to help them too much.

Others got back in various ways, some joining up with French soldiers or other English troops, some drove a horse and cart, others obtained bicycles and made their way to Dieppe.

In 1956 the 7th Battalion Royal Sussex Regiment was awarded the "Amiens 1940" Battle Honour for the stand it made at St. Roche.

> On the site where the 7th Battalion fell in Amiens, the Mayor has formed a memorial garden, with a magnificent granite cross war memorial.

Charles is buried in Abbeville Communal Cemetery Extension, Somme, France. Plot 9. Row F. Grave 5.

In this Commonwealth Cemetery there are 1754 from the Great War and 348 from the Second world War.

This scroll commemorates

Private Charles ATKINSON

The Royal Sussex Regt

held in honour as one who served King and Country in the world war of 1939-1945 and gave his life to save mankind from tyranny. May his sacrifice help to bring the peace and freedom for which he died.

St. Colmans Parish Churchyard

Bushmills Notes.

The funeral of Lieut.-Colonel Francis Salisbury Atkinson, late of the Royal Army Service Corps, took place on Monday to the family burying-ground attached to Derrykeighan Parish Church, Dervock. A large number of friends from Portballintrae, Bushmills, and Giant's Causeway attended to pay a last tribute of respect. The coffin, which was covered with the Union Jack, had been brought by motor hearse from Belfast, and was borne from the entrance to the church by six pall-bearers from Portballintrae and Giant's Causeway. The service in the neat little parish church was conducted by the Rev. S. Barnhill, rector, assisted by the Rev. F. Medcalf, Dunluce, and was most impressive. The hymns, "Onward, Christian Soldiers" and "O God, our Help in ages past," were solemnly and effectively rendered, being led by the choir. The service in the church over, the organ pealed forth the doleful "Dead March" in "Saul." The grave was specially prepared in moss, with settings of snowdrops. Buglers sounded the "Reveille," and after the service, which was conducted by the Rev. F. Medcalf, M.A., the "Last Post" was sounded. The late Colonel held a commission in the Inniskilling Dragoons, and formerly in the Queen's Royal Antrim Rifles. He saw considerable active service in the Egyptian Campaign, the South African War (1899-1902), and the Great War. For his services in the South African campaign he was graded D.A.A.G., and received two medals with six clasps.

Colonel Atkinson, whose Ulster house was Lissanduff, Portaballintrae, was the youngest son of Mr. Charles Robert Atkinson, M.Inst.C.E., and his wife, Ellen, daughter of Mr. Charles Douglas, of Dervock, was born at Windsor Avenue, Belfast, on March 7, 1869, so that he was almost 59 years of age. He was educated at Wall House, Malvern Wells, and Cheltenham College.

He was a grandson of Mr. Joseph Atkinson, of Malfield, Blackrock, County Dublin, whose wife, Sarah, was daughter of Baron George, one time Recorder of Dublin. His great-grandfather, Captain Joseph Atkinson, served in the French War and the American War of Independence, and was in 1791 High Sheriff of Dublin.

Colonel Atkinson married Violet, daughter of Mr. J. L. van Toll, of The Hague, by whom he had two sons.

As a sportsman he won the affection and esteem of all classes, and, prior to his disability, entered into the life and spirit of Portballintrae.

Amongst the many wreaths placed on his grave were the following:—"From Charles, Dennis, and Mrs. Atkinson"; "From Dr. and Mrs. Huey"; "East Cowes Football Club"; "Miss Ventnor"; "Miss Stewart, Ballyhivistock"; "Mr. and Mrs. Stuart-Moore and friends, Ballydivity"; "The Nursing Staff, Crossways Hospital, Osborne, I.O.W." The Royal Army Service Corps was represented by Colonel J. G. Lecky, C.B.E., who on behalf of the Corps placed a beautiful wreath on the grave. The chief mourners were—Mrs. Atkinson (wife); Mr. Charles Atkinson anl Mr. Dennis Atkinson (sons); and Dr. D. Huey, J.P. (brother-in-law).

At the morning service in Dunluce Parish Church on Sunday last the Rev. F. Medcalf, M.A., preliminary to his sermon, made touching reference to the death of Colonel Atkinson, whose family had been connected with Dunluce parish for over half-a-century.

Fred Wilkinson

Lance Corporal
6980126

2nd Bn., Royal Inniskilling Fusiliers

Died Thursday, 23rd May, 1940

age 20

Frederick Wilkinson was a member of the 2nd battalion of the Royal Inniskilling Fusiliers, who was born in Antrim but lived in Londonderry. His battalion was on home duties in training when war broke out.

In November 1939 his regiment was posted to the continent and took part in the fighting at that time. It was finally evacuated in May, 1940. Although the Battalion kept war dairies none of them survived for their time in France and Belgium. Mention of them is often made in histories of that time. They are quoted for example by the reverend Leslie Aiken in his book, Massacre on the road to Dunkirk. In this he records that a section of Inniskillings were involved in a

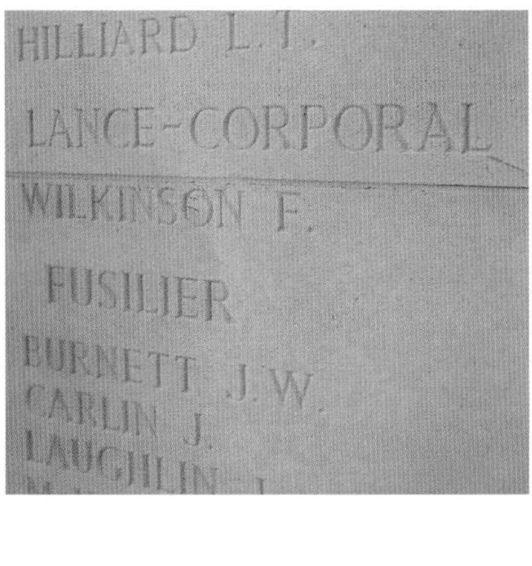

DUNKIRK 1940

Defeat and evacuation

When war was declared against Germany in September 1939, the 2nd Battalion of the *Royal Inniskilling Fusiliers*, just recently re-established, was sent to France as part of the British Expeditionary Force. (The 1st Battalion was stationed in India, and was there when war broke out against Japan in 1941.) The *5th Royal Inniskilling Dragoon Guards* had finally given up their horses and were mechanized in 1938, when they were equipped with Light tanks and Bren-Gun carriers. The regiment also joined the army in France where it was part of the Armoured Reconnaissance Brigade.

German Infantryman

The first nine months became known as the 'Phoney War'. Nothing much happened as the British army went into defensive positions in North West France. Then in May 1940 the Germans launched a massive attack called a Blitzgrieg, a devastating combination of armour, air assault and infantry attack. The British, French and Belgian armies, though well equipped, (their tanks were at least as good as the German tanks: the problem was in their deployment) they were unable to deal with this new form of mechanized warfare, and fell back in steady retreat. After many bruising encounters with the German army, the British army concentrated around the French channel port of Dunkirk. The Dragoons, after being involved in a successful counter-attack which slowed the German advance, drove their tanks and other vehicles to the water's edge, where they put them out of action. The men evacuated onto ships of the Royal Navy and safely reached home.

rearguard action at a place called Hal. Here they tried to stop the advance of the Germans by defending a canal bridge, which was also being used as an evacuation route. Because no accurate records of that time exist, the fate of Frederick is unknown. It is recorded that he has no known grave and his name appears on the Dunkirk memorial.

PANEL

" The war office has notified Mrs Matilda Wilkinson, that her son Lance-corporal Fred Wilkinson is missing, and Mrs Taylor has received intimation to the same effect regarding her son Jim. Both young men were serving with the Inniskillings, Fred Wilkinson's father Francis, also serving, had served in the great war "

Fred is also commemorated on Bushmills Presbyterian Memorial.

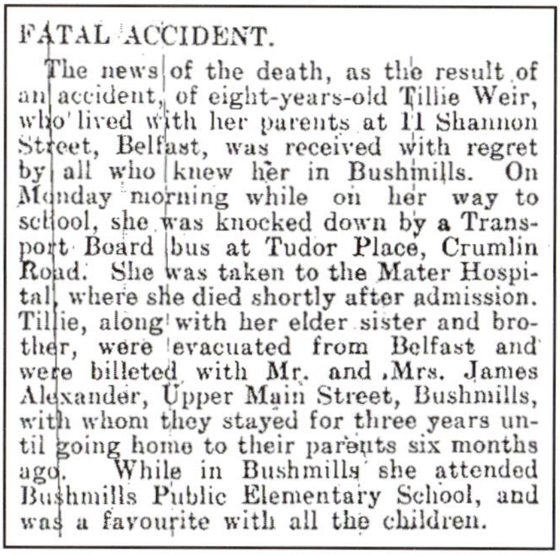

FATAL ACCIDENT.

The news of the death, as the result of an accident, of eight-years-old Tillie Weir, who lived with her parents at 11 Shannon Street, Belfast, was received with regret by all who knew her in Bushmills. On Monday morning while on her way to school, she was knocked down by a Transport Board bus at Tudor Place, Crumlin Road. She was taken to the Mater Hospital, where she died shortly after admission. Tillie, along with her elder sister and brother, were evacuated from Belfast and were billeted with Mr. and Mrs. James Alexander, Upper Main Street, Bushmills, with whom they stayed for three years until going home to their parents six months ago. While in Bushmills she attended Bushmills Public Elementary School, and was a favourite with all the children.

Thomas John Hanna

Private
5110616

2nd Bn., Royal Warwickshire Regiment

Died Tuesday 28th May, 1940

Age 23

Thomas John was the eldest son of Thomas and Alice Hanna. His siblings were, Margaret, William, Martha, Sara, Samuel, Theo, Daniel and James.

Thomas was born on 20th March, 1917. The eldest of a family of nine children. They lived at Ballynarris and attended Seneril Primary School. The family moved to Billy Cottages, 48 Haw Road where they remained until the death of William in 1992.

Thomas moved to England, and in 1937 he joined the Royal Warwickshire regiment from Leamington Spa. He was twenty years old.

He was on leave at home in 1940 for 6 days where he celebrated his 23rd birthday with his family. He later joined his regiment in England and was killed in the Dunkirk evacuation.

BUSHMILLS NOTES
SAT, JUNE 8th 1940

The gloom of sorrow passed over the town and district on Wednesday last on receipt of intimation from the War Office that a number of our gallant soldier lads are missing.

These include the son of Mr John Mckeague Orange Hall,

Alex McMullan Ardihennon, Thomas Hanna Castlecatt and William Rainey Revallagh. Dr. George Kane son of Mr and Mrs Frank Kane, Royal Hotel Giants Causeway, has been wounded

His brother Dan who retired after 32 years service in the R.U.C. can remember as an eight year old, the telegram boy bringing his devastated family the news that Thomas was missing in action.

Thomas's name is recorded on the beautiful Dunkirk Memorial. Column 41.

The Dunkirk memorial commemorates more than 4,500 casualties of the British expeditionary force who died in the campaign of 1939-1940 and who have no known grave.

Thomas is also commemorated on Billy Parish Church Memorial

"THE LAST MAN STANDING"

The 2nd Battalion Royal Warwickshire Regiment had gone to France on 24th September, 1939 through Cherbourg. They had gone to Rumegies where they had dug in. They built defensive positions including pillboxes.

In January 1940 they are on the move across Northern France, going to Metz

initially. In march 1940 they are at Waldweistroff. On 31st of that month they make their first direct contact with the enemy.

In April they are attacked and move off to Le Forest area. In May they begin fighting back. The battalion is bombed and shelled by the enemy.

On 25th May orders are received to withdraw to the Dunkirk area. On that day many of the unit are involved in a rearguard action, at a village called Wormhout. Many men are killed or captured.

No one knows for sure what happened to Thomas. It is now known that S.S. soldiers outside a little village called Esquebecq near Wormhout massacred many of the Royal Warwick's in a little barn. Thomas may well have been involved in this.

The 2nd battalion went on to land on Queen beach, a sub division of Sword Beach on 6th June 1944, d-day. They took part in the fighting around Caen

The story of what happened on that terrible day which was to follow remained unknown for a long time to the general public and historians.

Dunkirk Beach 1940

German soldiers viewing the tanks and armoured vehicles that the B.E.F. left behind.
The B.E.F. destroyed the vehicles to render them useless to the 'enemy'.

THE RETREAT TOWARDS DUNKIRK AND THE ORDER TO HALT THE ENEMY

The 2nd Battalion of the Warwicks on May 22nd start a long and difficult journey via Armentieres, Ypres then Poperinghe in Belgium on their way to Dunkirk. The exhausted battalion arrives in Wormhout where they receive the order to dig defensive positions around the commune with a view to fighting a rearguard action.

This scroll commemorates
Private Thomas HANNA
The Royal Warwickshire Regt

held in honour as one who served King and Country in the world war of 1939-1945 and gave his life to save mankind from tyranny. May his sacrifice help to bring the peace and freedom for which he died.

BUCKINGHAM PALACE

The Queen and I offer you our heartfelt sympathy in your great sorrow.

We pray that your country's gratitude for a life so nobly given in its service may bring you some measure of consolation.

George R.I.

"HOLD THESE POSITIONS TO THE LAST MAN AND THE LAST ROUND"

This was the task which fell to the 12th battalion. In other words, they were destined to make the sacrifice which would stop or delay the enemy and in doing so, would enable their comrades to escape.

The local people when they awaken, see the royal Warwicks stopped in the centre of the village. They wonder why, as the rest have already passed through on their way to the coast. Throughout the whole of the morning of May 27th troop convoys pass through Wormhout in a northerly direction, making for Dunkirk then suddenly just after midday, German planes drop their bombs on the centre of the village and in the area of the hospital. The red crosses painted on the hospital were ignored by the German pilots. The next day all hell broke loose, fighting bombing and explosions. The local people hid in their cellars, at 12.00 hours the resistance is fierce and many of the S.S. have been killed, their losses have been heavy. This maddened them, as up to now they had not met such defiance. Never since the beginning of the Polish Campaign had they met such resistance!

As the day went on the Nazis stepped up the pressure by constant reinforcements. Then they started taking their first prisoners. The battle was raging, dead and wounded littered the surrounding fields of Wormhout, the town was on fire, people were screaming in agony. So desperate was the British resistance from 14.30 hrs that the 3rd Panzer regiment almost gave up hope of any success.

MEMORIAL

Today near Wormhout, in that same field you can visit the site where the 2nd Battalion Royal Warwickshire regiment and others fought very bravely and died.

On November 9th 2001 two of the survivors were present when the barn which had been rebuilt, was dedicated.

After the massacre was over a local farmer nearby, under the cover of darkness and fearful that he may be seen by the S.S. filled a churn of milk and took it over to the barn for the soldiers to drink. He tried to help them, but for most of them it was too late.

A replica of the massacre barn today at Wormhout

That same churn is there today, a reminder of how brave the locals were in risking their lives for our soldiers.

This is a place of pilgrimage and refection.

THE MASSACRE OF THE WARWICK'S

May 1940 Flanders

The Geneva convention of 1929, whose signatories included Germany, stipulated in its article 23c;

"It is strictly forbidden to kill or injure an enemy who has laid down his arms or has no remaining means of defence and has surrendered".

In article 23d;

"It is forbidden to order that no quarter be given"

At Wormhout, the S.S. Leibstandarte Adolf Hitler, and in particular, the 2nd Battalion did not obey those laws. They gave no quarter.

On May 10th 1940, Hitler's divisions were mounting their cowardly attack on Holland and Belgium, and French troops and the British expeditionary force were moving directly to the area. Unfortunately for the allies, other German divisions were preparing to break through the unbreakable barrier of the Ardennes in order to attack from the rear.

On the evening of May 20th they had achieved the breakthrough and was about to reach Abbeville and complete the encirclement.

This German manoeuvre had succeeded perfectly and was cornering French and British troops in a trap.

Counter attack was impossible, the only salvation for the allies was an escape by sea, through the ports of Boulogne, Calais, Ostend and Dunkirk.

The Germans were advancing so rapidly and their resources so great that the only exit left was Dunkirk and nearby beaches.

Each successful day of embarkation from Dunkirk meant tens of thousands of fighting men saved from death or captivity.

It was essential to stop the German advance.

"This would be the task of a few

regiments or battalions, French and British. Sacrificing them could delay the Germans even by a day or a few hours enabling more soldiers to escape."

If the German soldiers had been from the regular army, then things could have been different, but................they were those fascists of Nazi ideology, none other than the S.S. Leibstandarte Adolph Hitler.

In the face of such an attack the Warwicks had only 3 options, death surrender or retreat.

'A' company whose H.Q. was at a farm was shattered by the onslaught of the Panzers. Many soldiers perished, many were captured.

The order was given to lay down their arms and the captain said to his brave men in the Warwicks,

"Don't be disappointed, you fought well"

The Nazi troops were by this time in a filthy temper and the majority were trigger happy. When a Capt. in the Warwicks took out his pistol in order to surrender he was shot to the ground. Wounded soldiers were shot at blank point range, other atrocities took place.

Calm slowly replaced the roar of the battle, then there was a violent storm and rain fell. The captured prisoners were marched away about 500 yards south of the church in Wormhout, there they were searched and mistreated, they were stripped of all their belongings including their identity discs, by the S.S.

They waited at this spot with their hands up for 15 minutes. They were wet, filthy, stinking, beaten, confused terrified and very uncertain of their future. They were in a state of shock at the murder of their comrades.

And so began the descent into hell . . .

For almost a mile the prisoners, some of them wounded, all of them tired, were forced to quick march into a field.

The prisoners arrived at a large field, with poplars all round, and in the corner was a small wooden shed, with a thatched roof, used as a byre for the cattle. A milk can was sitting at the main door.

More than 200 British Prisoners of War entered this field, *was this a prisoner assembly area* they thought ?

Captain Lynn-Allen tried to fight for better conditions for his men but he was refused.

The soldiers were forced into the shed, a grenade was thrown in. This confused the soldiers, many could not grasp what was happening. More grenades were thrown in, their flesh and limbs were broken and mutilated, the cries of the wounded doubled, the ground was covered with bodies, some still moving, others motionless . . .

The S.S. soon realised how ineffective the grenades were, they stopped, then they ordered the prisoners to come out. At first they didn't understand what they had to do. Then one said *"If we have to go outside, then lets go"* He was followed by four volunteers . . . they went out slowly, with dignity, heads held high. They reached a spot

twenty metres away and formed a line. An S.S. soldier armed with a rifle took his place behind each of the prisoners. Then they all understood what was about to happen and what the S.S. intentions were. They were forced to turn around.

Inside the barn, talking ceased and silence fell. Shots rang out one by one as the orders were called *"ein, zwei, drei, vier, funf!"* One by one the prisoners fell to the ground.

The S.S. came back to the barn and asked for five more volunteers. Once again they left the barn, they turned to face their executioners, eye to eye as the shots began again.

Killing all the prisoners five at a time would have taken a long time and another heavy rainstorm had started so they burst into the barn firing madly into the group of Warwicks. Then they trampled through the bodies spraying the barn with bullets. One soldier starting saying the lords prayer, the rest of the wounded and dying joined in, sadly most didn't get to finish. Many of the dying were gazing for the last time at photographs of a loved one that they managed to hide from the German searches.

When it was certain that the S.S. had gone away, those survivors, took stock of their situation. The butchery inside the barn was the stuff of nightmares.

Only eight men were able to leave the barn to get help — there were 15 survivors left.

"The sacred Tree"

A pollarded poplar dating from before May 1940. It was the nearest tree to the massacre barn, a cowshed destroyed in about 1960.

In 1972, British veterans who had fought in the area rediscovered the site and placed crosses there. It became a place of pilgrimage and proud witness to the thousands of veterans who come to pay homage to the victims.

Inside the 'replica' massacre barn at Wormhout

Memorial wreath and poppy cross left at the massacre site

Thomas Hanna's medals

Robert Daniel Maxwell

Driver T/ 166309

13 Troop Carrying Coy.,

Royal Army Service Corps

Died 28th May, 1940

Age 39

Mrs Maxwell Parkgate, Bushmills was officially notified by the war office in May 1942 that her husband Robert Maxwell, missing since the Dunkirk evacuation, is presumed killed.

Robbie was serving with the R.A.S.C. and was amongst the first in the Bushmills district to join up.

PROVEN, FRANCE
27TH MAY 1940

Early in the morning reconnaissance for a better location was carried out, and the company was finally located in three farms about half a mile apart from each other and about one mile north east of Proven.

They proceeded to Cassel and within two miles of reaching Cassel they came under heavy artillery fire and on enquiry from Welsh guards at the scene found out that the Germans had passed through Cassel.

They contacted the Section Commander of a supply depot,enquiring for advance G.H.Q. He could not give any information as he had been looking for them himself.

They then proceeded to Loos (24 miles) but could not find any traces of a H.Q. they then returned to Company Headquarters at Poperinge.

At this hour the stream of W.D. transport and other vehicles towards Dunkirk had become continuous and it was decided to change the location of the company to an area near Dunkirk. The company moved off by sections in the afternoon.

OUR HEROES-IN-MEMORIAM

IN LOVING MEMORY OF ROBBIE (DRIVER R.A.S.C.) PRESUMED KILLED IN ACTION BETWEEN 28TH MAY AND 2ND JUNE, 1940.

DEARLY LOVED HUSBAND OF NELLIE MAXWELL AND LOVING DADDY OF LILY, JIM AND BILLY.

5 BUSHFOOT COTTAGE, PORTBALLINTRAE.

ABSENT FROM THE HOME, BUT NEVER FROM THE HEART.

Commemorated on the Dunkirk Memorial to the Missing, column 137, Dunluce Parish Church Memorial

Portballintrae True Blues L.O.L. No. 1142

Dunkirk Memorial bears the names of 4507 men who died at the Dunkirk Evacuation and have no known grave.

PRISONER OF WAR.

Mrs. Maxwell has been notified through the Red Cross that her husband, Charles Maxwell, who was previously reported missing, is now a prisoner of war in Hong Kong. Charles is a son of Mr. Robert Maxwell, Portballintrae. His brother, Samuel, is a prisoner in Germany, and Robert, another brother, made the supreme sacrifice in France. Mr. Robert Maxwell, father of these three gallant young men, was, since the opening of the Bushmills and Giant's Causeway Tramway, employed by the company until about three years ago, and was one of the first to drive the old steam engines of those days prior to the inauguration of the electric system. Latterly he was in charge of the generating station at the Walkmill Falls on the River Bush.

BUSHMILLS NOTES

PRISONER OF WAR

MRS CHARLES MAXWELL, PORTRUSH, HAS RECEIVED A LETTER FROM HER HUSBAND, CHARLES, WHO WAS IN THE ROYAL NAVY, AND WHO HAS BEEN A PRISONER OF WAR IN THE FAR EAST FOR ALMOST TWO YEARS

HE STATES THAT HE IS WELL. THIS IS THE FIRST LETTER THAT HAS BEEN RECEIVED FROM HIM.

HE IS A NATIVE OF PORTBALLINTRAE. HIS BROTHER SAM IS A PRISONER OF WAR IN GERMANY. ANOTHER BROTHER ROBERT IS REPORTED MISSING, PRESUMED KILLED.

MR ROBERT MAXWELL, FATHER OF THESE THREE GALLANT MEN,WAS SINCE THE OPENING OF THE BUSHMILLS AND GIANTS CAUSEWAY TRAM-WAY, EMPLOYED BY THE COMPANY AND WAS ONE OF THE FIRST TO DRIVE THE OLD STEAM ENGINES OF THOSE DAYS PRIOR TO THE INAUGURATION OF THE ELECTRIC SYSTEM. LATTERLY HE WAS IN CHARGE OF THE GENERATING STATION AT THE WALKMILL FALLS ON THE RIVER BUSH.

DUNKIRK EVACUATION

A FEW FACTS

*338,226 Troops were evacuated from Dunkirk between 27th May and 4th June 1940.

*98,780 men were lifted from the beaches.

*239,466 from the harbour and mole.

*933 ships took part in operation Dynamo, of which 236 were lost and 61 put out of action.

*The number of little boats that sailed on their own initiative will never be known.

*French, Belgian Dutch and Norwegian ships took part in the operation, alongside the ships of the Royal Navy.

*The B.E.F. left the following equipment behind in France, much of it to be recycled by the German army.

2,472 guns,
63,897 vehicles
20,548 motorcycles
76,097 tons of ammunition
416,940 tons of stores

*68,111 men of the B.E.F. were captured or killed during retreat and evacuation.

*40,000 French troops were taken into captivity when Dunkirk fell.

*126 Merchant seamen died during the evacuation.

*Churchill had been Prime Minister for only 16 days when the evacuation began.

*The threat of invasion was so real that on 29th May, Churchill proposed laying gas along the beaches of the south coast.

*1,000 Dunkirk citizens died during the air raids on 27th May.

It seemed like a victory in just getting the troops back- over a third of a million of them – to fight another day.

BUSHMILLS.

L.O.L. No. 914 held its monthly meeting on Monday evening in the New Orange Hall, Br. Thomas Verner, W.M., in the chair, and Br. William M'Neill, D.M., in the deputy-chair. Two candidates were initiated.

At the weekly whist drive in the Men's Clubroom on Tuesday evening, Mrs. Grant, Bushmills, won the prize for the highest score. Miss M. Sinclair, Bushmills was first in the ladies' section, and Mr. F. C. Grant, first in the men's.

The recent heavy rains have caused the flooding of much land between the salmon leap at Walkmill and Benvarden. Potato pits are in many cases under water. Two fine days would result in a subsidence and little damage may be caused.

The response to the appeal made to the members of Dunluce Parish Church for funds to meet the expense of sending a Christmas parcel to the men from the parish who have joined H.M. Forces, has been eminently satisfactory, the amount subscribed to date being almost £31. Over seventy parcels will be forwarded. One member has made the supreme sacrifice, one is reported missing, and two are prisoners of war in Germany. Hopes are entertained of hearing about Robbie Maxwell, Bushfoot.

Harvest services in connection with Billy Parish Church were held on Sunday in the Giant's Causeway Schoolhouse. Billy Parish is one of the largest in the diocese of Connor and extends from the coastline south to Liscolman. The school at Giant's Causeway, opened twenty-five years ago, is a lasting memorial to the enterprise and benevolence of the late Lord Macnaghten, Runkerry, Runkerry being the title he took. The memorial sermon was preached by Rev. C. H. Walsh, Ballintoy. Miss Edith Martin presided at the organ, and the choir sang special hymns. Both services were conducted by the rector, Rev. W. J. N. Mackey, B.A.

Robert Maxwell's widow, Nellie visiting his Memorial at Dunkirk.

Speech by the Prime Minister, Mr. Winston Churchill, to the House of Commons on 4th June 1940, after the completion of Operation DYNAMO.

"Even though large tracts of Europe and many old and famous States have fallen or may fall into the grip of the Gestapo and all the apparatus of Nazi rule, we shall not flag or fail. We shall go on to the end. We shall fight in France, we shall fight on the seas and oceans, we shall fight with growing confidence and growing strength in the air, we shall defend our island, whatever the cost may be. We shall fight on the beaches, we shall fight on the landing grounds, we shall fight in the fields and in the streets, we shall fight in the hills; we shall never surrender, and even if, which I do not for a moment beieve, this island or a large part of it were subjugated and starving, then our Empire beyond the seas, armed and guarded by the British Fleet, would carry on the struggle, until in God's good time, the new world, with its power and might, steps forth to the rescue and the liberation of the old."

Robert's daughter Lily Montgomery and his son Billy at their fathers memorial at Dunkirk

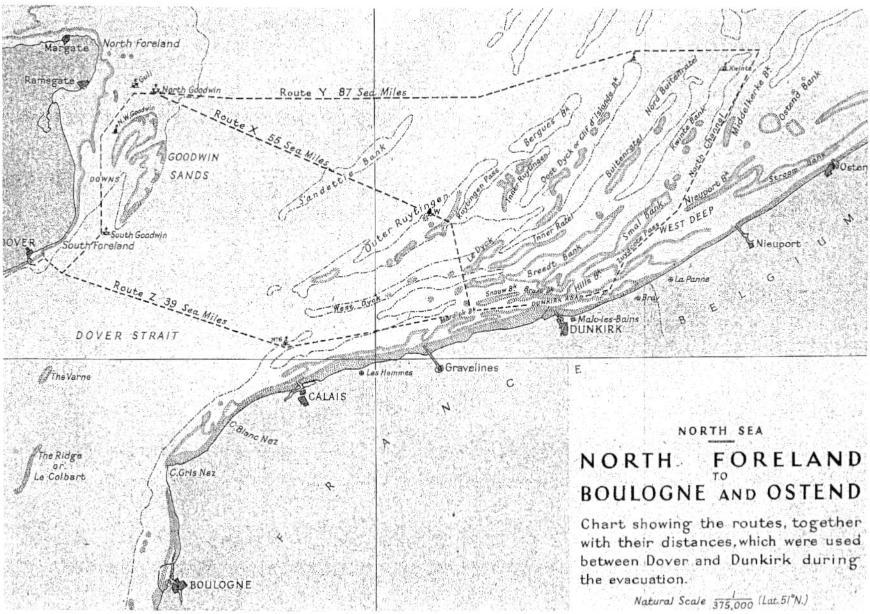

James Wilson McMullan

Sub-Lieutenant (E)

H.M.S. Foylebank
Royal Naval Reserve

Died 4th July, 1940

Age 36

Possibly the most intense action that Portland harbour experienced during its years as a Royal naval base, occurred in the early days of World War Two.

H.M.S. Foyle Bank was a converted 5500 ton merchant navy ship of the

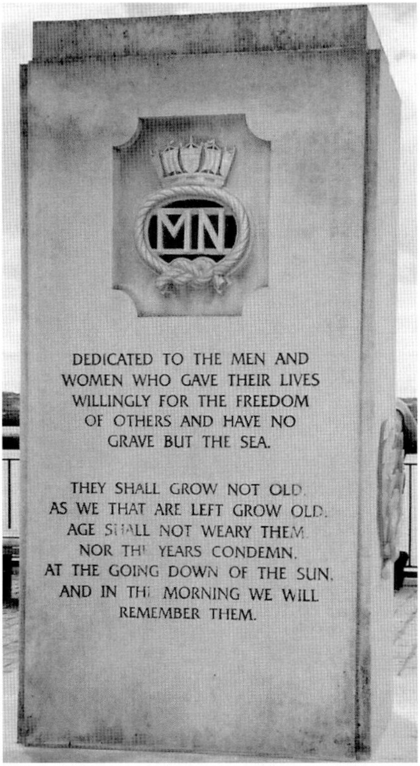

bank line. Launched in 1930 she was requisitioned in September 1939 shortly after the war broke out, and converted into an anti-aircraft ship with 2 pounder pom poms, 5 inch machine guns and 4 twin high angle 4 inch turrets.

She arrived in Portland on the 9th June work-up followed by anti-aircraft duties. On the 4th July, while the bulk of her crew were at breakfast, unidentified aircraft were reported to the south, but these were believed to be friendlies returning to base.

They turned out to be 26 of Germanys most feared aircraft,the JU 87 Stuka dive bomber, intent on getting the Foylebank.

The ship fought back and 2, possibly 3 Stukas were shot down,but 22 bombs found their mark and her guns were put out of action. Fires raged, electricity failed and the stricken ship listed to port, shrouded in smoke, she sank.

The action lasted a mere 8 minutes, during that time 176 men of the 300 man crew were killed and only 40 survivors remained uninjured.

The first V.C. ever to have been awarded in the U.K. was won here by leading seaman, Jack Mantle, who continued to serve his gun, though he was many times wounded.

LIVERPOOL NAVAL MEMORIAL

The Merchant Navy Memorial is situated on the Mersey River front at the pier head.

At the outbreak of war the Royal Navy knew that it would be impossible for them to man all the auxiliary vessels that would be serving with it.

To deal with this shortage, a number of officers and men of the Merchant Navy agreed to serve with the Royal Navy under the terms of a special agreement, which made them subject to naval discipline, while generally retaining their merchant navy rates of pay and other conditions.

TODAY'S POEM

For Merchant Navy Day:

HEROES

Don't speak to me of heroes until you've heard the tale
Of Britain's merchant seamen who sailed through storm and gale
To keep those lifelines open in our nation's hour of need
When a tyrant cast a shadow across our island breed.
Captains, greasers, cabin boys, mates and engineers
Heard the call to duty and cast aside their fears.
They stoked those hungry boilers and stood behind the wheel
While cooks and stewards manned the guns on coffins made of steel.
They moved in icy convoys from Scapa to Murmansk
And crossed the western ocean, never seeking thanks.
They sailed the South Atlantic where raiders lay in wait
And kept the food lines open from Malta to the Cape.
Tracked by silent U-boats which hunted from below,
Shelled by mighty cannons and fighters flying low,
They clung to burning lifeboats where the sea had turned to flame
And watched their shipmates disappear to everlasting fame.
I speak not of a handful but 30,000-plus,
Some whose names we'll never know in whom we placed our trust.
They never knew the honour of medals on their chests
Or marching bands and victory and glory and the rest.
The ocean is their resting place, their tombstone is the wind,
The seabirds' cry their last goodbye to family and friend.
Freighters, troopships, liners and tankers by the score,
Fishing boats and coasters, 2,000 ships and more
Flew the proud Red Duster as they sank beneath the waves
And took those countless heroes to lonely ocean graves.
Their legacy is freedom to those who hold it dear,
To walk with clear horizons and never hide in fear.
So when you speak of heroes, remember those at sea
From Britain's Merchant Navy who died to keep us free.

David Partridge, Botany Bay, Australia.
Submitted by shipmate George Hickman, Braunton, Devon.

The manning port to administer these men was at Liverpool. More than 13000 men served under these conditions in various types of auxiliary vessels, at first mainly in armed merchant cruisers, but also in armed boarding vessels, cable ships, rescue tugs and others on special service.

William Henry McMullan married Anne McAllister

Jane married James Cochrane

Anne
George
Mary

James Wilson
married Margaret Martin
KIA 4th July, 1940

Catherine Mary
married James White

Liverpool Naval Memorial

The memorial commemorates 1400 of these offices and men, who died on active service on board more than 120 ships and who have no grave but the sea. James Wilson McMullan is commemorated on panel 2 column 2.

James Sinclair

Ordinary Seaman

S.S Victoria City
Merchant Navy

Died 2nd December, 1940

Age 34

Copy of a letter sent to James's mother

Dear Mother,

We received your letter of January 15th yesterday, Saturday February 1st and were very sorry to hear about James. All of us since reading the newspapers on December 2nd about the nine ships that were sunk in convoy off the coast of Ireland and that S.S. Victoria was one of them. We were not sure if this was James's boat as it did not say S.S. Victoria City and James told us it took them 19 days to come over, so we all thought this was not his boat as he was supposed to have left on Saturday Nov 16 or 17th and he would not have time to reach the danger zone yet. We have been waiting word every day since hoping and praying it was not his ship.

This was the first letter Jane had received since you wrote and told us that we might expect to see James sometime soon. Although it is hard to write the following details we both know it will give you some pleasure to know how wonderful and happy was the time that he had with us all here and exactly what happened from the time he arrived until he left.

James arrived in Brooklyn, this is just across the river from NewYork city on November 9th and that night he tried himself to find our home so as to surprise Jane, but he got lost and had to return to the boat but mailed Jane a letter telling her where he was.

Monday was Armistice Day we did not get his letter until Tuesday morning. Jane called my place of business and left a message for me to call her and when I called her on phone she was so happy to tell me James was in America that she could hardly speak. I at once drove to the dock and got aboard the S.S. Victoria City and saw James, it was raining very hard and James was busy painting the boat, he asked his boss, Mr. Pinner if he could get off for the rest of the day and evening and he granted him leave at once. We then drove out about 25 miles to our house in the Country to Jane and the boys who were all waiting to see him and we all had a wonderful time.

The first thing James had was a hot bath, changed his wet clothes had supper and talked to all of us until mid-night, none of us wanted to go to bed and as our George has the best bed in the house,George would not let him sleep anywhere else.

Before he left for his ship on Wednesday morning George gave him a blue wool sweater, the first sweater his mother ever knitted for him while he was away at army camp in the summer and which he never had on. He gave this to James to keep him warm also a heavy leather coat of mine to help keep out the wind and rain and this fitted him perfectly and he was so pleased as it was very warm also a rain hat. Ron gave him all the magazines he could get into Georges suit-case, he had at the army camp and also gave him one of my Dunhill pipes which he got a great kick out of, carton of cigarettes and can of tobacco. Jane gave him a glass dish for you and one for his wife and compact for Lizzie as Jane did not have time to buy any Christmas presents, gave him money for his wife.

I drove back to the boat on Wednesday morning arriving at 7.30 a.m.and it was arranged that Thursday night our George was to show him around New York city while I was at work and he was to come out that night and sleep in our house he got such a great kick about George saying they would "paint the town red" , American slang for having a good time, but by Thursday night it was still raining

Towerhill Memorial to the Merchant Navy

and I guess James wanted to come to Jane's house and not waste any time seeing New York. He called me up at work and I arranged to get the night off and had his boss Mr. Pinner with him and asked if it would be alright to bring him along. Well!!! He could have brought the whole ship as they were all welcome at our house, anyway we arrived home about 7.30 p.m. and it was raining so hard you couldn't see but about 10 feet in front of you. Jane had supper for them and we all had a grand time.

During the evening James called up Rachel on the phone and joked with her about Willie and told Jane he had bought some little souvenirs for his wife and you and the rest of the family. While James was helping Jane wash the dishes Mr. Pinner his boss, I think that is how he spelt his name, who came from somewhere in the southern part of Ireland, spoke to me about James and said there was nobody he liked as well as James and was the only one he would go out with. He was about 27 and for the past 5 years was in charge of 16 of the crew of the 40 on ship. They were afraid they would get back to the other side to soon before Christmas and would be sent back before getting a chance to spend Christmas at home but made up that they would both spend Christmas together which ever home they could reach, either his or James and Jane told them that if they did miss Christmas at home, we would be waiting for them here with a big turkey, plum pudding and all the trimmings when they got back again.

Jane the boys and I were waiting for word and when it came it was a terrible shock to us all and we just can't believe and still hope that with God's will he is safe somewhere and we all will receive word soon from him, so we must have patience and pray for his safe return.

I forgot to mention that I drove them both to our house on Friday morning and left them at the boat at 7.30 a.m. and this was the last time I saw them both and there could be no happier two in the world. They could not thank me enough for the time they had.

I will try my best to find any information possible but I feel that James might have been picked up by some rescue ship or warship which has not reached port as yet.

Our George who thought the world of James and is exactly like him in his ways, told his mother last night that he was going to ask our Minister to say a prayer for James. So we were all there at the eight o' clock holy communion service and at the close of the service the minister said a wonderful.....most wonderful prayer for James and hoped we would receive word from him soon. He also personally spoke to both Jane and I leaving church, that he hoped that James was safe.

In closing, mother, Jane sent you a letter that must have been lost containing some snap shots of George when he was at army camp and one when James left, telling you that he was at our house but of course saying nothing more.

We hope and pray this letter reaches you and that you have received some word from James as to his whereabouts but if you have not, we will never give up hope for his safe return.

We have to be a brave family and carry on.

Thumbs-up

Love Jane, Wilson, George and Ronald.

TOWER HILL MEMORIAL

The tower hill memorial in London is the only memorial which commemorates merchant seamen exclusively.

It stands on a site near the tower of London and commemorates (Civilian) seamen of the mercantile marine (as it was known in the 1914-1918 war) and the merchant navy (1939-1945) war and fishing fleets who died as a result of the two wars and have no grave but the sea.

The First World War Memorial is linked to the Second World War Memorial by fights of stone steps leading into a sunken garden. The name of the 24,000 British and 50 Australian seamen are on bronze panels set against the retaining walls of the sunken garden.

*Locations of ships hit from convoy **HX-90**.*

The memorial was unveiled by Queen Elizabeth 11 on 5th November, 1955. There are 35807 names recorded from both wars

CONVOY BATTLES

Convoy Hx.90 Departed From Halifax / New York On 21st November 1940 and arrived Liverpool on 5th December 1940. Not all ships made it,

S.S. Victoria City was one of the 41 Merchant Ships on the Convoy which never made it home. Her cargo is listed as "General", at 4,739 tons.

On Dec 1st U-Boats are making a Patrol in the Western Approaches,the place where all homebound Convoys Pass. Three Convoys are approaching at the same time, one from Gibraltar the others from Cape Breton and Halifax / New York.

The U Boats find the Convoy before the Escorts do and make several attacks. With Good Sight-The Northern light is shining-and rough weather the U Boats penetrate easily and they can chose well their targets.

There were 7 U boats and 3 Italian boats involved in attacking Convoy Hx. 90 and U boat U-140 with Commander Hans-Peter Hinsch is credited with Sinking the S.S. Victoria City.

10 Ships sunk for a total of 57.556 Grt

1 Auxiliary Warship Sunk for a total of 16.402 Grt

4 Ships damaged for a total of 25.572 Grt

JAMES SINCLAIR FAMILY TREE

Archie married Margaret

Jane William Twins

Annie

James KIA David Twins

Jack

Minnie

Archie

Dan

Alex

Lizzie

Marjorie

James is commemorated on Ballintoy Parish Memorial

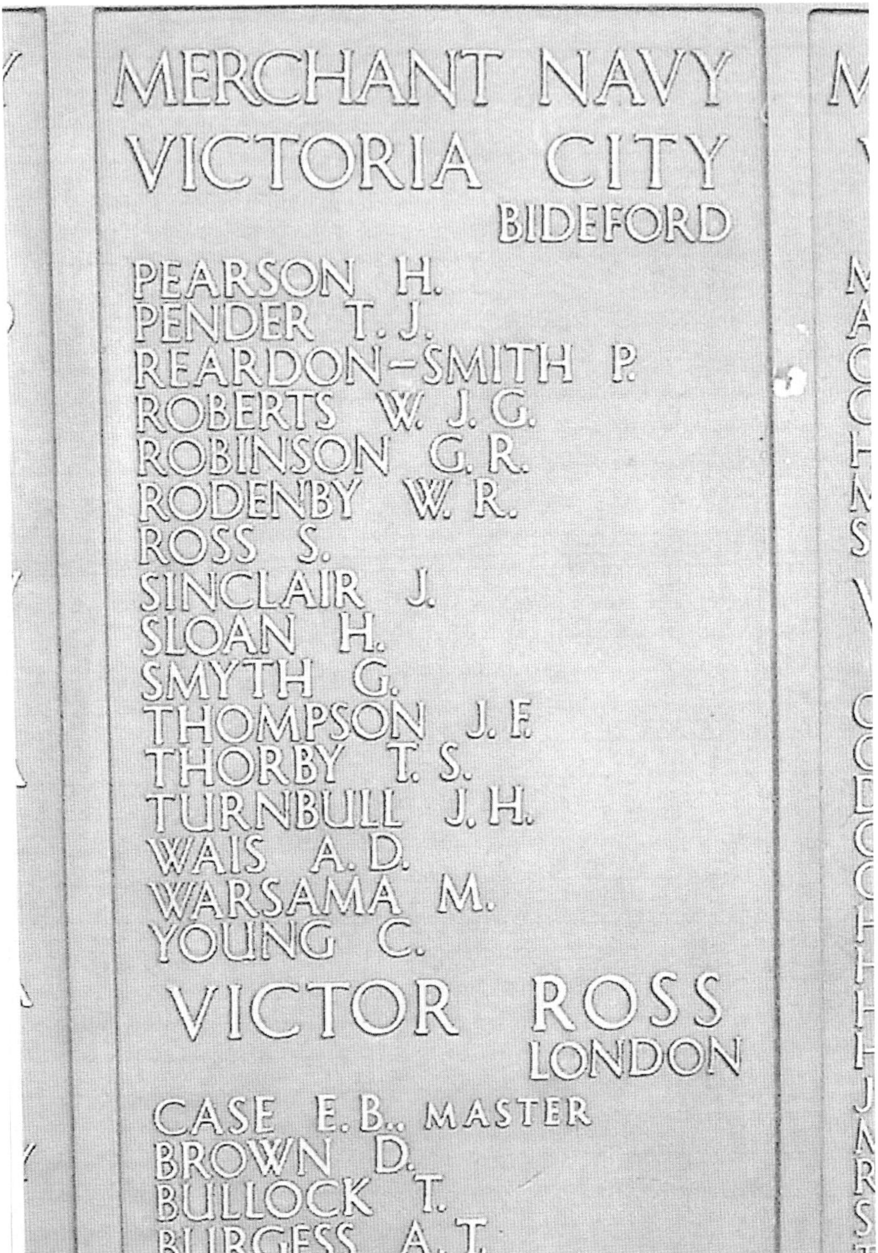
MERCHANT NAVY
VICTORIA CITY
BIDEFORD
PEARSON H.
PENDER T. J.
REARDON-SMITH P.
ROBERTS W. J. G.
ROBINSON G. R.
RODENBY W. R.
ROSS S.
SINCLAIR J.
SLOAN H.
SMYTH G.
THOMPSON J. F.
THORBY T. S.
TURNBULL J. H.
WAIS A. D.
WARSAMA M.
YOUNG C.
VICTOR ROSS
LONDON
CASE E. B., MASTER
BROWN D.
BULLOCK T.
BURGESS A. T.

Towerhill Memorial

Walter G Ascough

Guardsman 2719124

2nd. Bn., Irish Guards

Died Wednesday 4th December 1940

Age 19

Walter was the only son of William Walter and Olive Ascough, he had a sister called Dolly and they lived in Main Street Bushmills. William was a constable in the town during the war years.

> With deep regret the people of the town heard of the death of Guardsman Walter Ascough, aged nineteen of the 2nd Battalion Irish Guards, son of Constable Ascough, Bushmills, who was accidentally shot in England. His father and mother crossed to England when they got the news of his death. The sympathy of the entire community is extended to the family in their sad bereavement.

Walter was sitting on his bed writing a letter to his parents when he was accidentally shot.

He had previously been playing cards with his comrades, and had just sat down, and with his pen in his hand, he was fatally shot.

A corporal who was in charge of the soldiers when the accident occurred said he knew a Bren gun was in the room, but was not aware that there was any ammunition in it.

Guardsman Chalke who gave evidence in a low voice with some emotion said that he had been instructed in how to use a bren gun, he stated that he had not loaded it or attached a magazine to it. He had held up the gun, and while explaining that he was using it the next day, it went off.

There was no evidence as to who had attached the magazine. No one owned up.

Walter is commemorated on Dunluce Parish Memorial. He is buried in Brookwood Cemetery, London, England, Row 5 Section E Grave 2.

BROOKWOOD CEMETERY

During the two world wars, the United Kingdom became an island fortress used for training troops and launching land, sea and air operations around the globe.

There are over 170,000 Commonwealth war graves in the United Kingdom, many being those of service men and women killed on active service, or who later succumbed to wounds. Others died in training accidents or because of sickness or disease. They will be found in more than 12,000 cemeteries and Churchyards.

This scroll commemorates
Guardsman Walter ASCOUGH
Irish Guards

held in honour as one who served King and Country in the world war of 1939-1945 and gave his life to save mankind from tyranny. May his sacrifice help to bring the peace and freedom for which he died.

Brookwood is owned and cared for by the Commonwealth War Graves Commission. It is the largest Commonwealth Cemetery in the U.K. covering approximately 37 acres.

There are also cemeteries for American, Belgian, Czech, Dutch, French and Polish soldiers in Brookwood.

There are also German and Italian plots where prisoners of war are buried, not forgetting a plot for the Chelsea Pensioners.

BROOKWOOD MEMORIAL

The Brookwood Memorial commemorates 3,500 men and women of the land forces of the Commonwealth who died during the second world war in many lands, or at sea and have no known grave. The circumstances of their death were such that they could not be appropriately commemorated on any of the campaign memorials in the various theatres of war.

Francis Joseph Callaghan

Second Radio Officer

S.S. Koranton (Newcastle-On-Tyne) Merchant Navy

Died Friday, 28th March, 1941.

Age 23

Francis was the eldest son of Dan and Mary Ann Callaghan of Church Street, Bushmills.

His brother Dermont was also a wireless operator with the Merchant Navy and the ship on which he was travelling on his first voyage, was torpedoed. This was just 18 months after Francis was killed in action.

THE S.S. KORANTON

The S.S. Koranton left Halifax, Nova Scotia on 10th march 1941, with a load of pig iron bound for Hull, U.K.

On the morning of the 27th March 1941 she was half way between Canada and England, just south of Iceland, when she was torpedoed at

approx. 58N 22W by U-Boat U39. She sank immediately all 34 hands lost.

The U-Boat was commanded by Kptlt. Robert Gysae and its successes were 11 ships sunk at a total of 59.427 tons, and 1 ship damaged.

U-Boat U-98 was sunk on 15th November, 1942 in the north Atlantic west of Gibraltar by depth charges from the British Destroyer, H.M.S. Wrestler. All hands lost.

THE MERCHANT NAVY

During the second world war just under 4,8000 ships of the British Navy, their allies and neutral countries were sunk.

Total number of sailors who lost their lives was 32,000.

The Merchant Navy was often referred to as the "Fourth Service" or sometimes ruefully as "The Forgotten Service".

Francis is commemorated on Tower Hill Memorial, London. Panel 62

TOWER HILL MEMORIAL

The Tower Hill Memorial commemorates men and women of the Merchant Navy and fishing fleets who died in both wars and who have no known grave. It stands in Trinity Square, close to the Tower of London. There are 24000 names of sailors who have no grave but the sea.

Losses to the Merchant Navy reached their peak in 1942. The heaviest losses were suffered in the Atlantic. Convoys making their way to Russia around the North Cape and those supplying Malta in the Mediterranean were also vulnerable to attack.

In all 4,786 Merchant Ships were lost with a total of 32,000 lives, more than one quarter of this total were lost in home waters.

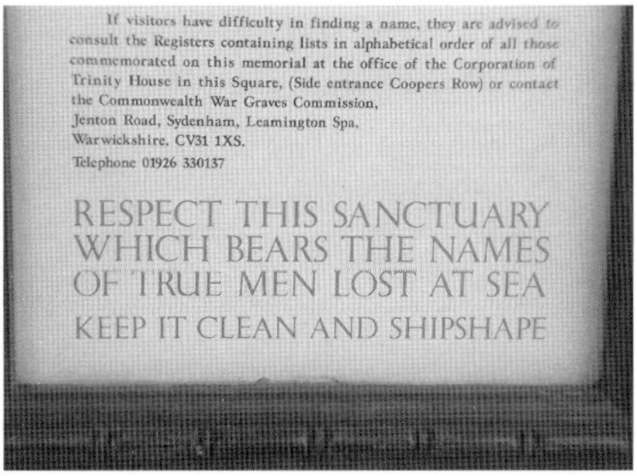

Robert Glenn

Petty Officer Stoker
P/KX 79270

H.M.S Hood Royal Navy

Died Saturday 24th May, 1941

Age 32

Robert Glenn was the only son of Margaret Glenn (nee Rodgers) and Archie Glenn from Ballinastraid. He had one sister Annie.

The Glenn Family had emigrated to America and after their mothers death, when they were quite young, their father sent them home to their mothers parents at Ballinastraid. They were brought up by grandparents Alex and Anne Jane Rodgers.

Annie had a son Gordon, who joined the R.A.F.

Robert joined the navy when he was 17 years old and had completed 15 years service when he lost his life on H.M.S. Hood.

Robert married Violet Rayner from Southsea in Ballintoy Parish Church.

His best man was Frank Kane and bridesmaid was Annie Wilkinson (Mrs Hoy).

Robert and Violet made their home in Southsea, Hampshire and they had one daughter Joan.

Robert or "Mickey" as he was known to his mates was H.M.S. Hoods official cartoonist. One of his cartoons was presented to Winston Churchill when he came on board the Hood on an official visit, also one was presented to King George.

After the war Robert planned to move to Malta, where one of the local papers had offered him a job as cartoonist.

Part of the crew of H.M.S. Hood

Boldre Church in New Forest, England

Roll of Honour in Boldre Church

With Ted Briggs, the last living survivor of HMS Hood

Robert was also a good singer and was part of the ships choir called the "Harmony Boys".

BALLINTOY SEAMAN'S DEATH

LOSS ON H.M.S. HOOD

Official notification has been received from the Admiralty that Stoker Petty Officer Robert Glenn is missing and presumed killed in action while serving on H.M.S. Hood.

Mr Glenn who was a grandson of Mr Alexander Rodgers, Ballintoy, entered the Royal Navy when 17 years old and had completed 15 years service.

For the past nine years he has served continuously on H.M.S. Hood.

His wife and daughter reside in England.

SHIPS, PROMOTIONS AND DATES

H.M.S. Victory *Stoker 2nd Class* 4th May 1928-3rd September 1928

H.M.S. Benbow *Stoker 2nd Class* 4th September 3rd May 1929

H.M.S. Benbow *Stoker 1st Class* 4th May 1949-6th May 1929

Emperor Of India *Stoker 1st Class* 7th May 1929- 22nd January 1931

H.M.S. Victory *Stoker 1st Class* 23rd January 1931-22nd January 1932

Royal Sovereign *Stoker 1st Class* 23rd January 19322nd August 1935

H.M.S. Victory *Stoker 1st Class* 23 August 1935-29th July 1937

H.M.S. Hood *Leading Stoker* 30th July 1937-11th June 1940

H.M.S. Hood *Chief Petty Officer* 12th June 1940- 23rd March 1941

H.M.S. Victory *Chief Petty Officer* 24th March1941-23rd March 1941

H.M.S. Hood *Chief Petty Officer* 24th March 1942- 24th May 1941

Robert is Commemorated In;
Ballintoy Parish Church
Bushmills War Memorial
H.M.S. Hood Memorial Church, Boldre, England

WHAT'S IN THE CAGE?

Sailor Glenn, home with the battle cruiser Hood after more than two years in the Mediterranean, walks along quay at Portsmouth with his wife and daughter Joan. But what's in the cage? Answer at foot of Column Four.

Archie Glenn Married Margaret Rodgers

Children
Robert Killed In Action 24th May 1941
Annie (Emigrated To California)

Cage mystery solved: canary for Joan, three weeks old when her father last saw her.

[illegible] of my darling [illegible] daddy of [illegible] H.M.S. Hood.— [illegible] wife Violet [illegible]
[illegible] I see you [illegible]
[illegible]
[illegible] I love [illegible]
[illegible]

Ballintoy Scroll of Honour

H.M.S. Hood

The Harmony Boys

PORTSMOUTH NAVAL MEMORIAL

Portsmouth Naval Memorial bears the names of 24585 men with no grave but the sea almost 15000 of these are from the Second World War.

Portsmouth Naval Memorial

Postcard sent home to his grandparents, Alex and Anne Jane Rodgers.

ELECTRIFYING NEWS

The sinking of the Bismarck, news of which electrified the world, was described in the House of Commons by Mr. Churchill.
His statement, was made to a very pleased house and came at a time when the loss of the British battleship Hood,
still cast a damper over the spirits of the public.
It was particularly gratifying, too, in that it was made at a time when there was news of British naval losses in the battle of Crete.
Mr Churchill concluded, "Great is our loss in the Hood, the Bismarck must be regarded as the most powerful, as she is the newest battleship in the world, and the striking of her from the German Navy is a very definite simplification of the task of maintaining the effective mastery of the northern sea, and the maintenance of the northern blockade.

Although there is shade as well as light in this picture, I feel that we have every reason to be satisfied with the outcome of this fierce and memorable naval encounter.

It is feared that there are very few survivors from the Hood, a battle cruiser with a displacement of 42,000 tons, she was the worlds largest warship.
She was built in John Browns shipyard on the Clydebank in 1916
And launched August 1918, completed two years later she cost about £6,025,000.
Her armament included eight 15 inch guns, twelve 5.5 inch, eight 4 inch anti aircraft guns, four three pounders, five machineguns and 10 Lewis guns.
In addition to multi-machine guns, four torpedo tubes and one aircraft.
The range of her biggest guns, firing a shell of nearly 2,000 lb.
Was 17 miles.

The Hood paid several visits to Northern Ireland waters, she visited Portrush in 1925

HER MOTTO WAS

VENTIS SECUNDIS
"WITH FAVOURABLE WINDS"

H.M.S. HOOD

On 21st May, 1941 the battlecrusier squadron of the home fleet, under the command of Vice Admiral Holland on his Flagship H.M.S. Hood, along with H.M.S. Prince of Wales and six other destroyers were ordered to the Denmark Straight between Greenland and Iceland.
On 22nd May 1942 the Bismarck and Prinz Eugen had been reported as having left Bergen, indicating an escape was imminent. At 7.45 p.m., on his Flagship H.M.S. King George V he led the rest of the home fleet towards the Denmark Straight. At 7.22 p.m. 23rd May, the cruiser H.M.S. Suffolk sighted the Bismarck and Prinz Eugen seven miles ahead of it in the Denmark Straight.
On 23rd May, the Bismarck and Prinz Eugen were sited 300 miles away from the Hoods force. The force increased its speed to 27 knots, and by 5.35 the next morning they were only 17 miles away. At 05.52 when the Bismarck was within 25,000 yards, the Hood opened fire, quickly followed by the Prince of Wales.
The Bismarck immediately returned fire, straddling the Hood with her second or third salvo, the magazine was hit and a fire broke out and quickly spread. At 16.00 hours just after the Bismarck fired her fifth salvo, a huge explosion split the Hood in two, and within a few minutes she had sunk. The Prince of Wales sent the signal "Hood sunk" which was received by the destroyer H.M.S. Electra at 16.00, and she and the rest of the escort instantly went on the search for survivors. H.M.S. Prince of Wales had to withdraw under the cover of smoke after being damaged, but was able to continue to shadow the German ship. The Bismarck had been hit and had sustained a fuel leak and headed for the fortified harbour of St. Nazaire.

The Bismark was hunted down and was sunk at 8.47 p.m. on 26th May. 110 men out of 2,000 of the Bismarck's crew were later picked up. Only three men out of the Hoods 1,421 men survived.

Ted Briggs is the only one still alive today, a very modest man. Never a day goes past when he doesn't think of his mates who lost their lives on.

"THE MIGHTY HOOD"

One of Robert's many cartoons

Ballintoy Parish Memorial

H.M.S. HOOD

WHEN H.M.S. HOOD WENT DOWN IN THE DEEP
THAT WAS THE NEWS, THAT MADE MOTHERS WEEP
FOR THEIR SONS WHO HAD FOUGHT, FOR A COUNTRY SO PROUD
WERE DOWN THERE BELOW, WITH THE SEA AS THEIR SHROUD
THEY SLEEP IN HEAVENLY PEACE, SLEEPING IN HEAVENLY PEACE.

THEN CAME GEORGE V, THE PRINCE OF WALES TOO
THEY TOOK A HAND, IN WHAT THE HOOD HAD TO DO
THE SUFFOLK, THE NORFOLK, THE COSSACK AS WELL
ALONG WITH THE RODNEY, SHELLED BISMARCK TO HELL
THEY SLEEP IN HEAVENLY PEACE, SLEEPING IN HEAVENLY PEACE.

SO MOTHERS AND WIVES, AND SWEETHEARTS BE PROUD
THOUGH YOUR DEAR LADS HAVE THE SEA AS A SHROUD
THEY WERE FIGHTING FOR FREEDOM, LETS NEVER FORGET
THE FREEDOM THEY FOUGHT FOR, WILL BE WON YET
THEY SLEEP IN HEAVENLY PEACE, SLEEPING IN HEAVENLY PEACE.

H.M.S. HOOD SUNK 21ST MAY, 1942 BY THE BISMARCK

IN MEMORY OF;

CHIEF PETTY OFFICER ROBERT GLENN BALLINASTRAID
LEADING COOK GEORGE B.B. SHEARER PORTRUSH

AND THE 1,418 WHO LOST THEIR LIVES ON H.M.S. HOOD

Alexander Rodgers Married Ann Jane (Montgomery)

- Margaret Jane married ArchieGlenn
  - Annie
  - Robert K.I.A. 21st May, 1941
- Samuel single
- Alexander married Euphemia Richardson
  - Margaret
  - Allister
- Mary married Dan Wilkinson
  - Ann Jane
  - Daniel
  - Jimmy
  - Akkie
- Archie married Marjorie
  - Beverley
  - Joyce
- William married Annie Kerr
  - Jean
- James married Emily Davidson
  - Norman
- Nancy single
- Mattie Single
- Rachel married Jim Dunlop
  - William
  - James
- Thomas married Rosetta Mcallister
  - Kathleen
  - James
  - Ann Jane
  - Thomas
  - Gerald
- Joseph married Dorothy
- Nora married Andy McKeown

William Smith

Petty Officer

D/JX 151875

H.M.S. Repulse Royal Navy

Died 29th December, 1941

Age 28

It was with deep sorrow that the relatives and friends of Petty Officer William Smith, heard of his death in the Far East.

The shock was all the more severe because of the fact some days previous, his family had been told that he was one of the sailors rescued from H.M.S. Repulse.

William was the son of Alexander and Sara Smith of Templastra and his brothers were Jim, serving in the R.A.F.,Robert, Archie and Mant, his sister was Mrs. Katie McLearnon.

William had served in the Navy for seven years, and was married to Mary, they lived in Lisbellnagroagh. He had previously served on H.M.S. Acastra and H.M.S. Revenge.

While on leave he liked to play football with his mates,Robert Glenn and Bertie McKay of Portbradden.

H.M.S. REPULSE

H.M.S. Repulse was laid down on 25th January, 1915 and completed August 1916.

Overall length 794.2 feet, 12000

horse power and a speed of 28.3 knots.

HER ARMAMENT IN MAY 1941

6 x 15 inch 42 calibre guns (3x2)

9 x 4 inch guns plus 6 x 4 inch anti aircraft guns

24 x 2 ponder a.a. guns

8 x 21 inch torpedo tubes.

Compliment of 1180 men

MOTTO

Qui Tangit Frangatur
(Whoever touches me, breaks)

H.M.S. REPULSE

H.M.S. repulse was a renown-class battle cruiser, the second to last built by John Brown and Company, Clydebank, Scotland.

She was considered to be a high maintenance ship and was given the nickname "H.M.S. Repair" and her sister ship, Renown known as H.M.S. "Refit".

After the outbreak of war the Repulse operated on various hunting groups, mainly to hunt down German commerce raiders. At the end of the year she performed escort duty for troop carriers between Canada and Britain. At the start of the Allied Campaign in Norway the Repulse was involved in mine laying by the British forces.

In 1941 Repulse participated in the hunt for the German Battle Cruiser, Scharnhorst and Gneisenau. Then in

Kranji War Cemetery

In Memory of

Petty Officer WILLIAM SMITH

H.M.S. Repulse, Royal Navy
who died aged 28 on Monday, 29th December 1941.

Petty Officer SMITH was the son of Alexander and Sarah Smith, of Bushmills, Co. Antrim, Northern Ireland; husband of Mary McWhirter Smith, of Bushmills.

Remembered with honour
KRANJI WAR CEMETERY, Singapore.

In the perpetual care of
the Commonwealth War Graves Commission

May she took part in the chase for the Bismarck, which had just sank H.M.S. Hood and losing his life on that ship was his friend, Robert Glenn.

In August she was transferred to Cape Town, South Africa, then in October to India.

At the end of 1941, as the threat of war with Japan loomed, Repulse was detached to the Far East as a deterrent to further Japanese aggression. On 8th December 1941 after the outbreak of the war in the Pacific, H.M.S. Repulse left Singapore with other major elements of the British fleet, the fast battleship the Prince of Wales and 4 destroyers to intercept Japanese convoys heading towards Malaya.

On 10th December after failing to find any Japanese forces, and turning south, Japanese aircraft were spotted.

The fleet was attacked by 86 Japanese aircraft based in Saigon, attacking both ships, Prince of Wales and Repulse.

The Repulse managed to dodge 19 torpedoes before being sunk in 20 minutes after receiving 5 torpedo hits.

H.M.S. Electra and H.M.S vampire moved in to rescue the survivors of the Repulse while H.M.S. Express rescued survivors of the Prince of Wales.

Some survivors of the Repulse manned action stations on Electra to free the sailors, so that they could rescue more survivors. In total 1285 survivors of the Repulse were rescued, Electra rescued 571 of these, 327 perished.

William is buried in Kranji War Cemetery in Singapore after being killed in a flying accident. Section E Row 10 grave 35 beside sailors from H.M.S. Repulse.

He is commemorated on Dunseverick Church Memorial.

R.B.P. MEETING

The "William Johnstone" Memorial R.B.P. No. 559 held its monthly meeting in the Orange Hall. Sir .Knt. James McKeague W.M. presiding, with sir. Knt. Arthur McElnay, D.M. in the Deputy Chair.

The W.M. moved, in feeling terms, the sympathy of the Preceptory with Sir. Knt. Alexander Smith, Templastra, whose gallant son William lost his life on active service in the far east.

The motion was passed in silence.

KRANJI WAR CEMETERY

Kranji War Cemetery lies 22 kilometres north of the city of Singapore, and overlooks the Straights of Johore.

On the 8th February, 1942 the Japanese crossed the Johore Straights, landing at the mouth of the Kranji River, within two miles of where the cemetery now stands.

The Kranji area was a military camp before 1939 and at the time of the Japanese invasion of Malaya, it was a large ammunition magazine.

The Bridge over River Kwai

After the fall of Singapore the Japanese established a Prisoner of War camp at Kranji and eventually a hospital.

There are 4458 commonwealth war graves here, and a massive Memorial to the missing, with the names of over 24000 men who have no known graves.

OUTSTANDING WAR DATES OF 1941.

DURING 1941 the war spread through the entire Continent of Europe and across the world. The following are the dates of the principal extensions of the war and of subsidiary campaigns:—

April 6—Germany invades Greece and Yugoslavia without warning. Athens entered on 27th April.

May 2—Fighting breaks out in Iraq between British forces and pro-Axis Iraqui troops.

May 20—Landing of German air-borne troops in Crete. Allied withdrawal from Crete announced on June 1.

June 2—British troops enter Baghdad; armistice granted.

June 8—Allied forces enter Syria.

June 22—German troops invade Russia, striking through Baltic States, Russian-occupied Poland, and, with Rumanian troops, into Bessarabia.

July 14—Syrian armistice signed at Acre.

August 25—British and Russian troops enter Iran.

November 18—Beginning of the second Libyan offensive.

November 27—Gondar, the last Italian stronghold in Abyssinia, surrenders.

December 6—Britain declares war on Finland, Rumania and Hungary.

December 7—Japan enters the war. She attacks the U.S. Pacific bases without formal declaration, and the High Command states later that Japan has been at war with Britain and the U.S. since dawn.

December 8—Britain, the U.S. and the Netherlands Empire declare war on Japan.

December 9—China at war with Japan —officially.

December 11—Germany and Italy declare war on the U.S., and the U.S. replies at once with declarations against the Axis.

PORT BRADDAN

PORT BRADDAN, backed by scrubby cliff, is based
On rock, sure founded, though the oceans roar
And foam against its foot;
By boundless, restive waters ever faced
And waves that would approach the very door,
Their spume eaves-high to shoot.

The winds that wander from the farthest dark
Across the floods, wail weirdly as they come
To harass this grim coast,
To eddy in the crevices, the stark
Rock columns echoing like rolling drum
Or hollow sounding post.

The chimney with the blast reverberates,
The smoke is torn and beaten as it flies
Such tumult to escape;
The grey gull seeks to join his scattered mates
That make the wild day wilder with their cries;
Stones upon black stones scrape.

Nor'westers come on sunwashed summer day
With great cloud-galleons across the blue;
And white waves, lifting tall
As ships with fluttered canvas, fill the bay.
To the tired world, her spirit to renew,
They call and louder call.

Along the sands the yellow moonlight gleams,
And velvet-black the heights their shadows cast;
And where they silent loom,
Flow bubbling from the hanging rock the streams—
Such tiny things!—that, laughing, bid the vast
Sea solitudes, "Make room!"

The sands are lonely underneath the stars;
The waves but whisper as they mount the beach
And backward gently slide;
The rollers seem as motionless dark bars;
Yet evenly, each swelling after each,
They shoreward glide.

The full-orbed moon rides slowly through the sky,
The stars, revolving on their ordered way,
Their watch in heaven keep;
The houses, huddling by the sea-cliffs high,
That flank the curving shores of Whitepark Bay,
In shadowed silence sleep.

BRIAN McALISTER

The
COMMITTEE
Representing Ballintoy and District
'In Memoriam'
1939 - 1945
Realising the magnitude of the services and sacrifices to our country and to the World by those who served in H.M. Forces, Q.A.I.M.N.S. and Merchant Navy during the second World War, your friends and neighbours wish to express their deep regret and sympathy to the relatives of
P.O. Wm. Smith, R.N.
who made the supreme sacrifice to King and Country.

William's brother Jim's scroll from Ballintoy

In all the war I never received a more direct shock. As I turned over and twisted in bed, the full horror of the news sank into me.

Winston Churchill on hearing of the loss of the *Prince of Wales* and *Repulse*.

An early photograph of 'Repulse'

John McGauhey

Sergeant
6977694

The Royal Inniskilling Fusiliers

Died 30th January, 1942

Age 28

Sergeant McGauhey along with eight other soldiers, drowned when their flat bottomed collapsible boat was swamped. They were on a training exercise in an Northern Ireland Bay when the accident happened.

The men had gone out in their small boat to cross a narrow strip of water when they got into difficulties.

After the boat had been caught broadside, the water poured into her. The men made frantic attempts to get the bow of the boat head-on to the waves, but they were unsuccessful.

They were thrown into the water, and a few minutes afterwards disappeared below the surface.

Another boat which was some distance away, endeavoured to reach the scene, while a lance corporal who witnessed the tragedy, dived into the water and swam out towards the boat. He was picked up in an exhausted condition by another boat which had set off from the shore.

Sergeant McGauhey was seen by an eye witness standing up at the stern, presumably to get the men to row together, as he was heard to shout "in out in out"

Accidental death was the verdict.

Sergeant John McGauhey was buried in Billy Parish Church and is commemorated on their war memorial.

MILITARY HONOURS AT FUNERAL

The funeral of Sergeant McGauhey, formally of Turfahun, Bushmills took place on Sunday to Billy Parish burial ground. The funeral was one of the largest ever seen in the neighbourhood. There was much sympathy felt for his wife and little daughter Shirley, only two years old.

Full Military Honours were accorded.

The pall bearers included comrades of the unit to which John was attached and members of the public who carried the coffin draped with the Union Jack, the entire distance from Turfahun to the church. Members of the local detachment L.D.V. were also present.

Rev. W.J.N. Mackey B.A. rector of Billy officiated at the graveside. There was a firing party and the "last post" was sounded.

Amongst the wreaths placed at the graveside were several from his comrades, with whom he was very popular.

Mrs McCaughy received a letter from the commanding officer in which he says *"May I extend to you and your family the very real sympathy of the officers, N.C.O. and the men on the death of your husband, Sergeant McGauhey. Your husband was a really good soldier and very highly though of by myself, his company officers and the men whomhe trained with such keenness. He will be missed by all of us and will indeed be hard to replace".*

The bodies of seven of the men were taken to England for burial, as their families had asked for them to be buried at home.

Fusilier W. F.H. Harris of Monmouthshire was buried in Tyrella Church of Ireland.

THE RIFLES THE SKINS AND THE BOLD FUSILIERS

WHEN THE WAR DRUMS HAD SOUNDED THE CLANS TO THE CALL
THREE BRAVE IRISH REGIMENTS WERE THERE ON THE BALL
THEY LANDED IN AFRICA TO CLASH WITH THE HUN
AND CAME OUT IN GOOD TIME TO MISS NONE OF THE FUN
THEY JUMPED INTO ACTION, WITH THREE HEARTY CHEERS
DID THE RIFLES, THE SKINS AND THE BOLD FUSILIERS.

HAW-HAW IS A LIAR, A TRUTH YOU'LL ADMIT
HE SAID THAT OUR LADS, WERE NOT DOING THEIR BIT
BUT THEY'LL DASH HITLER'S HOPES AND THEY'LL CROWN GOERINGS FEARS
WILL THE RIFLES, THE SKINS AND THE BOLD FUSILIERS.

A TANNER WAR PAY IS NOT MUCH YOU'LL ADMIT
BUT IT HELPS ALL THE LADS OUT THERE DOING THEIR BIT
IT HELPS TO BUY FAGS AND A FEW EXTRA BEERS
FOR THE RIFLES THE SKINS AND THE BOLD FUSILIERS.

ON A HILL CALLED TANGAUCHA THEY OPENED THEIR SHOW
AND SOON FROM THAT HILL JERRY QUICKLY DID GO
THEY HOISTED THE WHITE FLAG THROUGH THEIR DEADLY FEARS
OF THE RIFLES, THE SKINS AND THE BOLD FUSILIERS.

WHEN LONGSTOP HAD FALLEN, WE KNEW WE'D HAVE FUN
TO THE PLAINS WITH OUR RIFLES WE FOLLOWED THE HUN
WE MARCHED INTO TUNIS THE FRENCH GAVE US THREE CHEERS
FOR THE RIFLES, THE SKINS AND THE BOLD FUSILIERS.

AS WE MARCHED IN THROUGH TUNIS HEADING STRAIGHT FOR CAP BON
THE FRENCH IN THEIR THOUSANDS CRIED "LES ANGLIS, TRES BON"
THEY CRIED WITH DELIGHT, ALL THE WOMEN IN TEARS
TO SEE
THE RIFLES
THE SKINS
AND THE BOLD FUSILIERS.

David Esdale

Sergeant

R.A.S.C.

Argyle And Sutherland Highlanders

Died 23rd February 1942

EX SOLDIERS DEATH

We regret to announce the death of another townsman in the person of Mr David Esdale, in his 60th year, who after an illness of almost a year, passed away at his mothers residence, Main Street, on Monday of last week.

"Davie" was a member of a highly respected family, his father and he having carried on business as bakers prior to his joining the Army in 1901.

He served for twelve years with the R.A.S.C., being discharged in October, 1913.

When the Great War, 1914-1918 broke out, he re-enlisted and was on active service until discharged in May, 1920.

After the outbreak of the present war, he again re-enlisted on July 11th, 1940. And served until 6th June, 1941, when owing to failing health, he was discharged.

He served with the Argyle and Sutherland Highlanders during this last period of service to his King and country.

In the interval between the Great War and the present war, "Davie" was actively engaged for a period in training "B" Specials, holding the rank of Sergeant Instructor.

The funeral to Ballywillan burying-ground was largely attended by all creeds and classes. The coffin was draped with the Union Jack, and comrades of the British Legion marched at each side of it as the funeral left the town.

Rev. R.H. Kimber, M.A., conducted the services in the house and at the graveside.

The chief mourners were-Messrs. Charles Esdale (son) William, Daniel, Samuel and Patrick (brothers), William Sinclair and Charles Sinclair (uncles) Pat Irwin, Thomas Sinclair, William, Samuel, Peter and Joseph McCloskey (cousins)

Ballywillan old burial ground

Allan Lamont

Able Seaman
D/SSX 17853

H.M.S. Jaguar Royal Navy

Died 26th March, 1942

Age 26

Alan Lamonts sister Mrs Maggie Patton gave me a cherished photograph of her brother Allan, it was very dear to her as it was to her mother Mrs. McLean, and brother William of Store Row Bushmills.

Allan joined the navy 1936 age 20, he had been with the navy in the far east and fought in Norway at the battle of Narvik. He was wounded at the Dunkirk evacuation, but not before helping a local soldier.

Robert Miskelly of Ballydivity was serving in the royal artillery and his unit was waiting at Dunkirk on the beaches to be evacuated. When his turn came he got into difficulties in the water and thought he was going to drown, when, a sailor reached down and pulled him out. That sailor was Allan Lamont, Roberts brother the late John Miskelly told me of how his brother Robert and Allan became friends and tried to keep in contact.

Sadly, Robert died at the hands of the Japanese 13th May, 1943 and is commemorated on Kranji Memorial, Singapore.

H.M.S. JAGUAR

During the evacuation at Dunkirk, H.M.S. Jaguar picked up 700 troops. When returning to pick up more on the 29th May, she was attacked by 17 dive bombers. H.M.S. Jaguar fired back and damaged one, which was finished off by a fighter. She was attacked later that afternoon and her engines and steering were put out of action. She was towed into port.

One D.S.C two D.S.M's and 12 Mentioned in Despatches were awarded to the ship for this action. She continued to operate in home waters until she left the Clyde for Gibraltar with H.M.S. Renown and others where she carried out escort and patrol duties with Force H. She took part in the shelling of Cherbourg with the battleship H.M.S Revenge and later was in action with the Italian Fleet of Cape Spartivento.

H.M.S. Jaguar then took part in the covering of a convoy from Gibraltar to the Eastern Mediterranean, and arrived at Malta with H.M.S. Illustrious which had been damaged by bombs. Later on in 1942 she took part in intercepting Vichy ships.

On 3rd of april she was ordered to port Said with H.M.S. Janus as four enemy destroyers were reported heading northwards of Port Sudan.

In May H.M.S. Jaguar took part in the battle for Crete in which she was one of the few ships to escape damage. The following month she was back with Force H during the Syrian Campaign. The next she was involved in Operation Guillotine conveying R.A.F. personnel to Cyprus from Port Said. From then to October she operated off the Libyan coast bombarding the Bardia area.

On 20th December she rescued 8 officers and 17 ratings from the destroyer H.M.S. Kandahar which had struck a mine off Tripoli.

During the first three months of 1942 she continued with the 14th destroyer Flotilla carrying out escort duties in the Mediterranean. She then meets a convoy setting out from Alexandria on its way to Malta while serving with Force K.

On 26 the March 1942 while escorting the RFA Oiler Slavol, with supplies for Tobruk, she was torpedoed and sunk by u boat u-652 North of Sollum. Eight officers and 45 ratings were rescued by the anti-submarine Whaler KLO but three officers and 190 ratings lost their lives. One was Allan Lamont of Bushmills. Not long after the same U boat sank the Slavol.

On 2nd June 1942 a British swordfish aircraft badly damaged the u boat u-652 in the Mediterranean in the gulf of Sollum. The U-boat was then scuttled with 46 survivors and no casualties.

Allan's family were devastated when they got the news that he was missing in action, and hoped that he would return. This was not to be and a year later they were told that he had

been killed in action The family continued to remember Allan by putting these beautiful verses in the local paper.

Short was your life, my darling son
Tis sweet to breath your name,
In life I loved you very dear
In death I do the same.

Ever remembered by his loving mother Store Row.

I felt it hard I had to part
With one I dearly love
But there's a thought that cheers my heart
That we shall meet above
Your end was sudden Allan dear
You made me weep and cry
But oh! The saddest fact of all
We never said goodbye.

Always remembered by his loving sister, Margaret and brother William

Two years has past since that sad day
When one I loved was called away
Forget him? No I never will
As time rolls on I love him still

Allan is commemorated on Plymouth Memorial, Devon Panel 65 column 3 and also Dunluce Parish Church Memorial.

Valetta Harbour, Malta

HMS Jaguar

HMS Jaguar, a destroyer of the Javelin class, was authorised under the 1936 programme. She was laid down at Denny Bros. yard at Dumbarton, Scotland on 25th November 1937, launched on 22nd November 1938 and completed on 12th September 1939.
After trials she joined the 7th Destroyer Flotilla in the Humber Force at Grimsby on 26th September. In the space of the next two months she was twice attacked by enemy aircraft but sustained no damage. She was employed mainly on anti-submarine patrols and escort duties off the East Coast until the end of 1940. On 20th May 1940 she was in the force which cut the six telegraph cables between the East Coast and Borkum and Nordeney (Operation Quixote) returning to Yarmouth next day.

HMS Jaguar (captained by Lt Cdr J F W Hine, RN), during the evacuation from Dunkirk.
After evacuating 700 troops on the 28th May 1940 HMS Jaguar was returning to pick up more when, at 11:55 am on the 29th May, she was attacked by 17 dive-bombers. She damaged one, which was later finished off by a fighter. She was attacked again at 3pm and holed near the waterline by a near miss, putting her engines and steering out of action. After some time under tow repairs were effected and she reached port under her own power. One DSC, two DSMs and 12 Mentioned in Despatches were awarded to the ship for this action.

She continued to operate in Home Waters until November when she left the Clyde for Gibraltar with the HMS Renown and others where she carried out escort and patrol duties with Force H. On 11th October she took part in Operation Medium, the shelling of Cherbourg, with the battleship HMS Revenge and destroyers of the 5th Flotilla and MTB's. On 27th November she was in action with the Italian Fleet off Cape Spartivento.
Early in January 1941 she took part in Operation MC4, the covering of a convoy from Gibraltar to the Eastern Mediterranean, and on 10th arrived at Malta with HMS Illustrious which had been damaged by bombs during the operation. Later that month she also took part in Operation Ration, the interception of Vichy (enemy French) ships.
On the night of 27th/28th February she assisted in covering the landing of troops at Castelorizo, in the Dodecanese, and during the withdrawal had a slight engagement with the Italian Destroyer Crispi. On 3rd April she was ordered to Port Said with HMS Janus as four enemy destroyers were reported heading northward off Port Sudan. These destroyers, however, were deterred by aircraft from HMS Eagle.
In May HMS Jaguar took part in the battle for Crete in which she was one of the few ships to escape damage. The following month she was in Force H during the Syrian campaign. During July she was one of the ships which conveyed RAF personnel to Cyprus from Port Said, Operation Guillotine, and for the next few months operated off the Libyan coast, bombarding the Bardia area in October.
On 20th December she rescued 8 officers and 17 Ratings from the destroyer HMS Kandahar which had struck a mine off Tripoli. The Kandahar was eventually sunk by a torpedo from Jaguar.
During the first three months of 1942 she continued with the 14th Destroyer Flotilla carrying out escort duties in the Mediterranean, and on 18th January, she is part of Force K, which meets a convoy which had set out from Alexandria for Malta on 16th, and escorts it back.

On 26th March 1942, while escorting the RFA oiler Slavol, with supplies for Tobruk which were to be used to refuel the 5th Destroyer Flotilla, she was torpedoed and sunk by U652 (Kapitaneutnant Georg-Werner Fraatz) in position 31'53N-26'18E, north of Sollum/Sidi Barrani. Eight Officers and 45 Ratings were rescued by the anti-submarine (a/s) whaler Klo but three Officers and 190 Ratings lost their lives. Not long afterwards U652 sank the Slavol.

Sources:
Naval Historical Branch, Newspaper Reports, British Warships Losses of the 20th Century, Paul Kemp

U-652

Type:		VIIC	
Laid down:		5 Feb, 1940	Howaldtswerke, Hamburg
Commissioned:		3 Apr, 1941	
Commander:		3 Apr, 1941 - 2 Jun, 1942	Georg-Werner Fraatz
Career:	8 patrols	3 Apr, 1941 - 30 Jun, 1941	3. Flottille (training)
		1 Jul, 1941 - 31 Dec, 1941	3. Flottille (front boat)
		1 Jan, 1942 - 2 Jun, 1942	29. Flottille (front boat)
Successes:		5 ships sunk for a total of 11.450 tons	
		3 ships damaged for a total of 20.835 tons	

Fate: Badly damaged by depth charges from a British Swordfish aircraft and scuttled on 2 June, 1942 in the Mediterranean in the Gulf of Solum, in position 31.55N, 25.11E, by torpedoes from U-81. 46 survivors (No casualties).

Samuel Mckeague

Private
6981153

Pioneer Corps

Died 12th June, 1942

Age 33

"A wave of sorrow spread over the town and district when it became known that Private Samuel Mckeague third son of Mr and Mrs John Mckeague of the Orange Hall Bushmills, had been killed by accident. He was in training in Scotland, having joined the Gordon Highlanders and later transferred to another regiment. He had been home on leave shortly before, and only a few days before his death his mother had a letter from him stating that he was well. It was not disclosed in the telegram how he met his death.

The body arrived at Portrush railway station and was conveyed to Bushmills, being met by his father and two brothers and other friends. The funeral was to the family burying ground at Dunluce Parish. It was largely attended.

All the business houses in Bushmills were closed and all blinds were drawn as the cortege passed up Main Street and Church Street. The military provided the pall bearers.

The last post and reveille were sounded at the graveside.

Rev. R.H. Kimber officiated."

Private J.McCroskery of the Pioneer Corps, a native of Belfast was acquitted and discharged at Dundee on a charge of the culpable homicide of Private Samuel McKeague, by discharging a loaded rifle at him as he was playing the organ in a Church Hall at Angus, where the soldiers were billeted.

While Samuel was playing the organ, a shot was heard and McCroskey was seen with a rifle in his hand. The two men were close friends and always went on leave together.

McCroskey said in evidence that Samuel began to try and play the organ. He made plenty of noise and witness jokingly called him "Reginald Foort" he then lifted his rifle, put a round in it, applied the safety catch, and pointed it above Samuels head. He then intended to take out the cartridge, and in doing so his finger must have been on the trigger and the gun went off. It was an accident".

In loving memory of our dear son samuel who was killed on active service in Scotland.

Still ours in memory, thoughts and love.

Sadly missed by his loving mother, father sisters
Serving in the Middle East
The Hall, Bushmills.

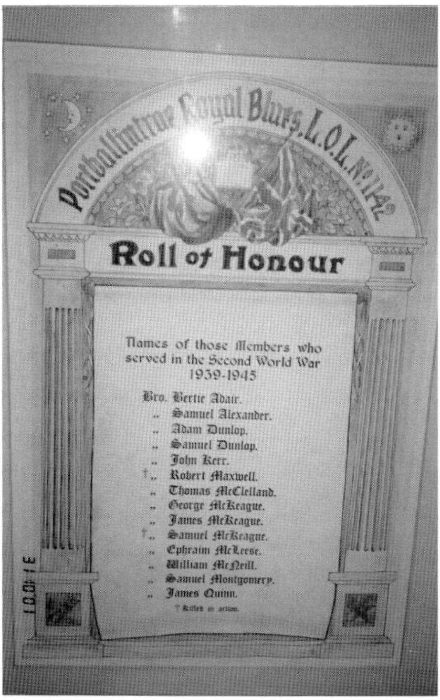

Beautiful memories are all that is left.

Ever remembered by his loving sister, brother in law Jean and William Alexander also little nieces Muriel and Elizabeth, Church Street Bushmills

Time may pass and bring its changes
Fresh with every coming year
But his memory will be cherished
By the hearts that hold him dear

Ever remembered by his brother Thomas and sister in law Bella and nieces and nephews, Messines House, Bushmills.

Samuel is commemorated on Dunluce Parish Memorial and Portballintrae Royal Blues L.O.L. No. 1142

At the quarterly meeting of Busmills District L.O.L Br. Trevor H. Willis W.D.M. Presiding with Br. James Wilkinson D.D.M. in the Vice Chair offered their sympathy to the McKeague family.

The initial cap badge

James McAlister

Petty Officer
P/SSX 15157

H.M. Submarine P 514
Royal Navy

Died 21st June, 1942

Age 27

James was the only son of James Hill and Katherine McAllister and brother of Rosetta (Mrs Tommy Rodgers).

Jim was born in Ballinastraid, Bushmills. He married Ina Bennett from the Feigh and they had one son called Robert James, who died in infancy and is buried in Dunseverick Parish Church.

Jim joined the Royal Navy at the age of 19 and had completed eight years service when the submarine that he was stationed on was sunk. He had served on H.M.S. Resource and H.M.S. Revenge in the Mediterranean fleet before joining the submarines.

The submarine that he was serving on when he died was P 514. They were of the coast of Newfoundland when they were accidentally rammed and sunk in error by the Minesweeper H.M.C.S. "Georgian".

The submarine was launched in 1918 in America and had been handed over to the Royal Navy under the lend-lease agreement in 1941. On 9th March 1942 she entered the Royal Navy where she spent her days operating with the Royal Canadian Navy, largely in the capacity of a training vessel.

On 20th June 1942 she sailed from the fishing village of Argentia on Canada's eastern seaboard escorted by the Flower Class Corvette, Primrose. She was routed along the "safest inshore route" to St. Johns, Newfoundland 65 miles to the north. On 21st June 1942 she encountered one of her own convoys and was rammed and sunk with all hands lost. There were 32 ranks and ratings on board.

Except for the Corvette Primrose, no vessel in the area knew that P 514 was at sea. Georgian had assumed that the dark shape crossing her bows was an enemy. An attempt to locate and possibly rescue survivors was put in hand, but failed after many attempts.

Jim's mother Katy received "the telegram" notifying her that her son was lost at sea, Sadie Rodgers was with her at the time as were most of her neighbours.

His nephew Jimmy Wilkinson could remember Jim being home on leave and he had grown a beard as there were no shaving facilities on board the submarine.

Willie Moore of Tonduff married Ina and they emigrated to Canada.

Jims name is on Portsmouth Naval Memorial Panel 62. He is also commemorated on his family headstone in Toberkeigh Presbyterian Churchyard.

While serving in the navy he wrote often to his mother Katherine, he also sent home postcards and photographs of the places he had been to while serving in the Navy.

I remember as a young child, she would take out an old box tied up with a ribbon, and tell me about her son Jim and show me her precious memories.

Family grave, Toberkeigh Presbyterian

Sweetest memories of our darling brother, Jim
Petty officer. Who lost his life on H.M. submarine p 514 June 1942

He sleeps beside his comrades
in a spot to us unknown
His name is written in letters of love
In the hearts that he left at home

Always in the memory of his loving sister and brother in law Rosetta and Tommy Rodgers Main Street Bushmills.

Two loving hands are resting
The voice we loved is still
The uncle we lost is waiting
for us just over the hill

Remembered lovingly by his nephews and nieces, Kathleen,Jimmy, Anna, Tommy and Gerald.

We watched the boys around come home
We watched for our son in vain
We now realise with a broken heart
He won't ever return again

Ever will be remembered by his devoted father and mother James Hill and Katie McAlister Ballinastraid.

I don't forget you darling
Nor do I intend
I will think of you always
And will to the end

Deeply regretted by his sorrowing
wife Ina McAlister

James Hill McAllister Married Katy Glass (Rathlin Island)

Jim (KIA 21/6/42) married Ina Bennett — James (died in infancy)

Rosseta married Thomas Rodgers — Kathleen, James, Ann Jane, Thomas, Gerald

Ex-American "R" class: Three unnamed (P.511/512 & P.514).

These old ex-American boats were transferred to the Royal Navy in 1941/42 principally for training, but were occasionally used operationally as convoy escorts. They were of single-hull Holland design, and were slightly larger than the contemporary British "H" class.

Displacement: 530 tons (590 full load surfaced/684 submerged tons).
Dimensions: 179 (wl)/186¼ (oa) × 18 × 18d/12¼ (13¾ full load) feet.
Machinery: Two shafts, NLSE ...cyl (bore ...in × ...in stroke) diesel engines BHP 880 = 13½ knots surfaced + Electric Dynamics electric motors SHP 934 = 10½ knots submerged.
Bunkers & radius: O.F. 60 tons, 3,700/.....nm @ 10/...k surfaced/2 × ...-cell battery .....AHr, .../...nm @ .../...k submerged.
Armament: One 3in gun; four 21in (all fwd—four reloads) T.T.
Complement: 33.
Diving depth: 200 feet.

Above and below: The ex-American submarines *P.512* (above) and *P.511* (below). (NMM/IWM)

Pt. No.	Name	Builder (Hull)	Builder (Engine)	Laid down	Launched	Completed	Fate
Acquired ../../41							
P.511	Unnamed ex-*R.3*	Fore River Shipbuilding (Quincy)	New London Shipbuilding & Engineering	11.12.17	18. 1.19	17. 4.19	Returned USN 20/11/44, foundered Kames Bay 27/11/47, salved ../12/47; sold West of Scotland Shipbreaking 10/12/47, arrived Troon 21/2/48 for scrapping.
P.512	Unnamed ex-*R.17*	Union Ironworks (San Francisco)	-do-	5. 5.17	24.12.17	17. 8.18	Returned USN 6/9/44; sold American shipbreakers 16/11/45, arrived Philadelphia ../../45 for scrapping.
P.514	Unnamed ex-*R.19*	-do-	-do-	23. 6.17	28. 1.18	7.10.18	Rammed in error RCN minesweeper GEORGIAM en route Argentia/St Johns 21/6/42.

"THE TELEGRAM" FROM THE WAR OFFICE

missing, presumed killed while on war service.

In order that information may be denied to the enemy, it is not at present possible to make public details of the operations during which your son became a casualty, and I must ask you, therefore, to refrain from disclosing to those who do not already know it, the name of your son's ship and to regard as confidential until such time as an official announcement can be made, anything beyond the fact that your son is missing, presumed killed while on war service.

There can, I fear, be no hope that your son is still alive and I should, therefore, like to express, on behalf of the officers and men of the Royal Navy, the high traditions of which your son helped to maintain, sincere sympathy with you in your sad bereavement.

Yours sincerely,

Commander,
for COMMODORE (on leave)

Mrs. Katherine McAllister,
White Park,
Bushmills,
Co. Antrim,
N. Ireland.

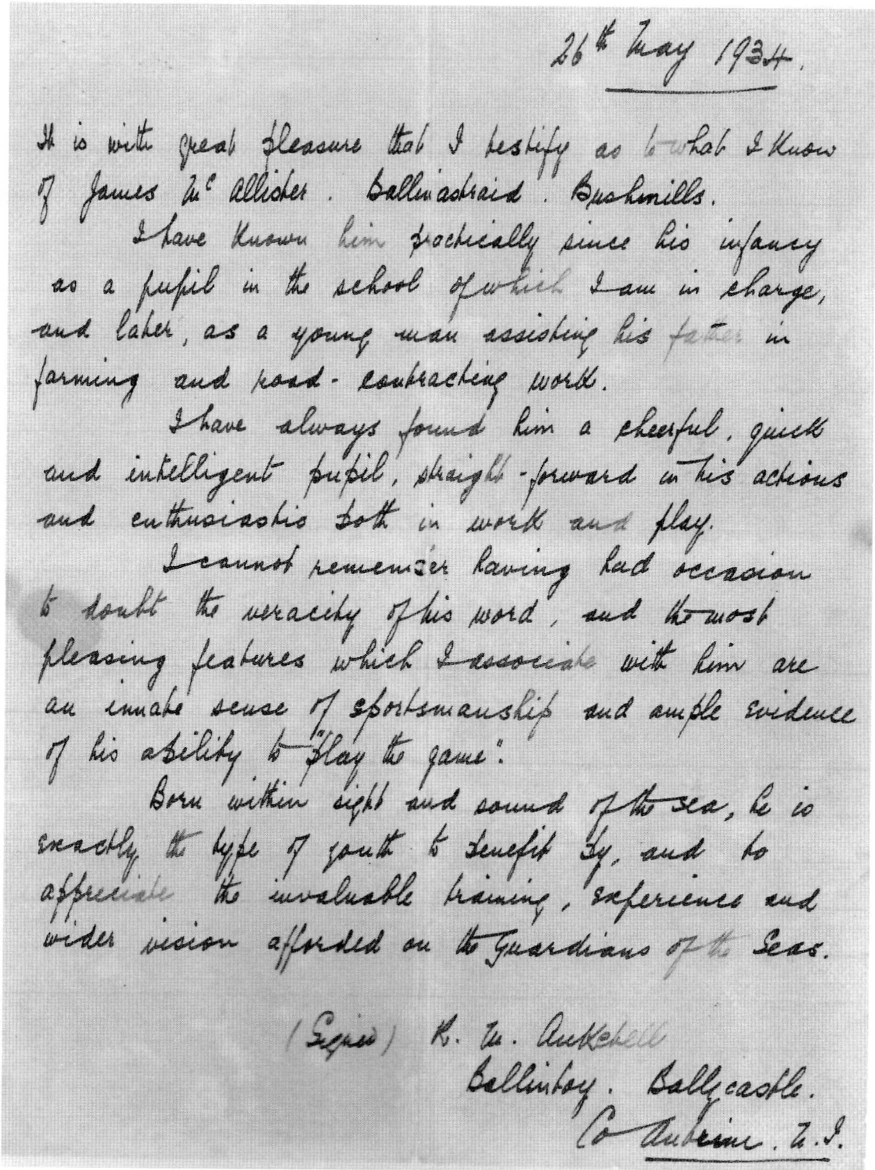

26th May 1934.

It is with great pleasure that I testify as to what I know of James McAllister. Ballinastraid. Bushmills.

I have known him practically since his infancy as a pupil in the school of which I am in charge, and later, as a young man assisting his father in farming and road-contracting work.

I have always found him a cheerful, quick and intelligent pupil, straight-forward in his actions and enthusiastic both in work and play.

I cannot remember having had occasion to doubt the veracity of his word, and the most pleasing features which I associate with him are an innate sense of sportsmanship and ample evidence of his ability to "play the game".

Born within sight and sound of the sea, he is exactly the type of youth to benefit by, and to appreciate the invaluable training, experience and wider vision afforded on the Guardians of the Seas.

(Signed) K. M. Anketell
Ballintoy. Ballycastle.
Co Antrim. N.I.

A reference for Jim to join theNavy by the Principal of Ballintoy School, K.M. Anketell

The
COMMITTEE
Representing Ballintoy and District
'In Memoriam'
1939 - 1945
Realising the magnitude of the services and sacrifices to our country and to the World by those who served in H.M. Forces, Q.A.I.M.N.S. and Merchant Navy during the second World War, your friends and neighbours wish to express their deep regret and sympathy to the relatives of
P. O. Jas. McAlister, R.N.
who made the supreme sacrifice to King and Country.

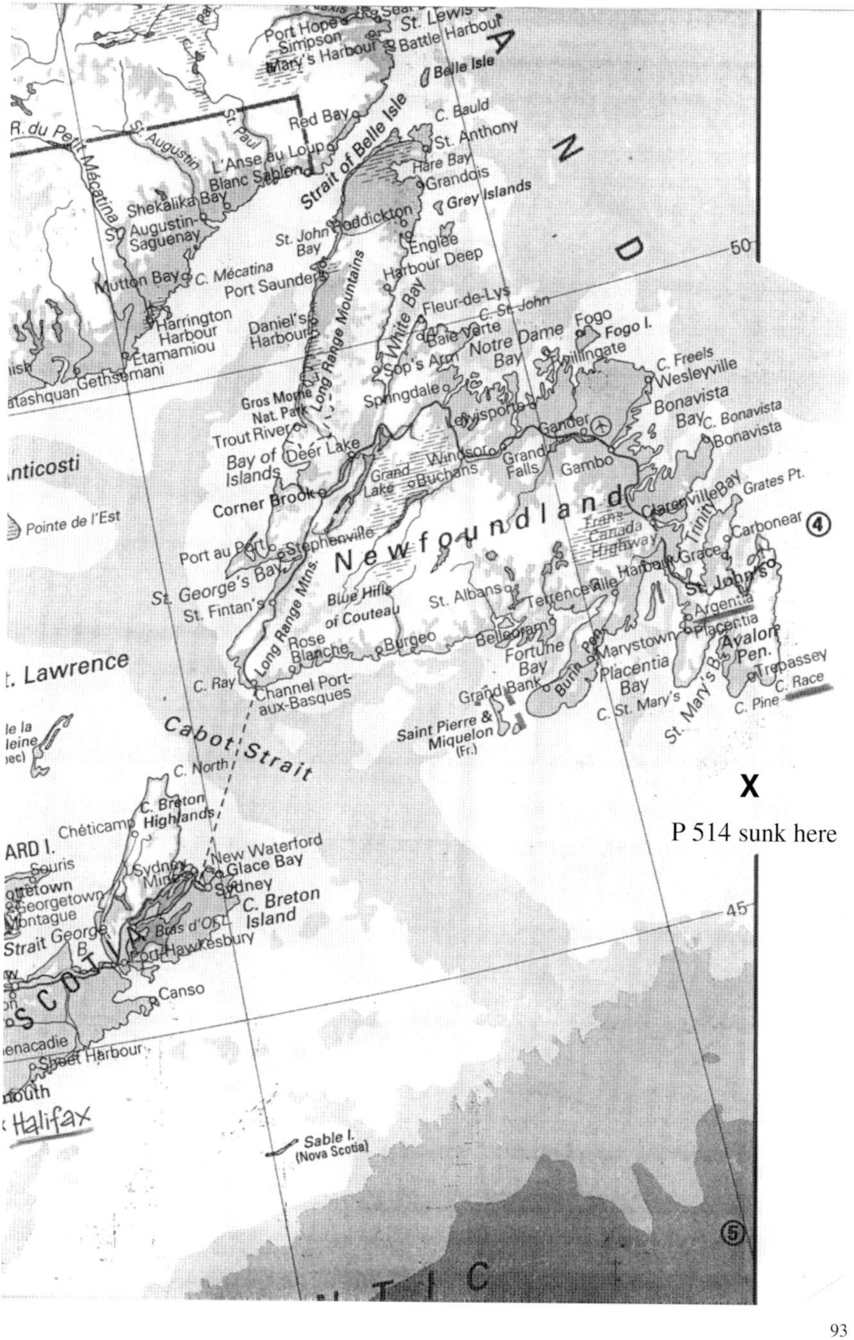
Port Hope Simpson
Mary's Harbour
St. Lewis
Battle Harbour
Belle Isle
Red Bay
C. Bauld
St. Anthony
R. du Petit Mécatina
St. Augustin
St. Paul
L'Anse au Loup
Blanc Sablon
Strait of Belle Isle
Hare Bay
Grandois
Shekatika Bay
St. Augustin-Saguenay
Grey Islands
St. John Bay
Roddickton
Englee
Harbour Deep
Mutton Bay
C. Mécatina
Port Saunders
Long Range Mountains
White Bay
Fleur-de-Lys
C. St. John
Harrington Harbour
Daniel's Harbour
Baie Verte
Fogo
Fogo I.
Etamamiou
Notre Dame Bay
Twillingate
Gethsemani
Sop's Arm
C. Freels
Wesleyville
Gros Morne Nat. Park
Springdale
Lewisporte
Bonavista Bay
C. Bonavista
Bonavista
Trout River
Gander
Bay of Islands
Deer Lake
Windsor
Grand Falls
Gambo
Anticosti
Grand Lake
Buchans
Corner Brook
Clarenville
Trinity Bay
Grates Pt.
Pointe de l'Est
Newfoundland
Trans Canada Highway
Carbonear
Port au Port
Stephenville
Harbour Grace
St. George's Bay
Long Range Mtns.
Blue Hills of Couteau
St. Albans
Terrenceville
St. John's
St. Fintan's
Argentia
Rose Blanche
Burgeo
Belleoram
Marystown
Placentia
Avalon Pen.
St. Lawrence
Fortune Bay
Burin Pen.
Placentia Bay
Trepassey
C. Ray
Channel Port-aux-Basques
Grand Bank
C. St. Mary's
St. Mary's B.
C. Race
C. Pine
Cabot Strait
Saint Pierre & Miquelon (Fr.)
C. North
C. Breton Highlands
X
P 514 sunk here
Chéticamp
New Waterford
Glace Bay
Souris
Sydney Mines
Sydney
Georgetown
Montague
C. Breton Island
Strait George
Bras d'Or L.
Port Hawkesbury
Canso
Sheet Harbour
Halifax
Sable I. (Nova Scotia)
45
50

To my dear
Mother
From your loving Son

to my dear Mother

J. McALLISTER.
H.M.S. "Revenge,"
Mediterranean Fleet.
All
Good Wishes

Joseph Watters

Royal Ulster Rifles
and No. 4, Commando

Died Wednesday, 19th august 1942

Age 26

I never met my Dad for when I was born during the Second World War he was at Weymouth, Dorset with No. 4 Commando preparing for the Dieppe Raid.

He was killed in that action.

The information that I am about to impart was gleaned from family, friends and former members of No 4 Commando.

This story was researched and told by Jim Watters, Troon Ayrshire

My father Joseph Watters was born in Bushmills, Co. Antrim, Northern Ireland on 24th May 1915. His father, James and mother Mary (nee McMullan) had moved to Bushmills from Seneril a few miles away.

Joe was educated in Bushmills, and, on leaving school, served an apprenticeship with McMichaels the butcher, Main Street Bushmills. He was a keen amateur footballer and a much-respected goalkeeper for Bushmills Rangers.

Joe had five siblings, two older sisters, Martha and Anne, a younger sister, Maisie, a younger brother, David and the youngest of the family, a sister, Lillie.

The family were members of the Presbyterian Church in Ireland. They lived in a large house adjacent to the Church in Upper Main Street, Bushmills. Their father, James served as sexton of the Church and even helped the Minister in the preparation of sermons. Their mother, Mary cleaned the Church and was active in its social side. James made the Roll of Honour that hangs in the Church to this day and now bears the name of his son, Joseph. James was also the foreman in the "Old Bushmills " whiskey distillery and my information is that he was t-total.

My fathers younger sister, my aunt Lillie spoke of the times when Joe worked at the butchers and would sneak off with the shops message bicycle, collect her from school and carry her home on the bar. She was and still is, very fond of her big brother.

In his late teens, Joe joined the regular army enlisting with the 1st battalion, Royal Ulster Rifles at Ballymoney.

He saw service with the 1st Battalion in China and India. In India he acquired the nickname "Pawny" this being the Indian word for water. This nickname would remain with him for the rest of his life.

After the withdrawal from Dunkirk in 1940, the First Lord of the Admiralty, Winston Spencer Churchill, called for the formation of a guerrilla force "a special type of soldier". Thus the Commando was formed.

They had to be volunteers and battle hardened. They had to be extremely fit and able to work in all conditions. They had to be able to work as part of a team or on their own initiative.

Joe volunteered.

The initial interview, according to John (J.E.D.) Price, was pretty gruelling and lengthy. A member of the interviewing board was a Royal Army Medical Corp Officer whom John later learned was a psychologist, so covering all aspects of a mans ability to carry out the type of work the Commando would be asked to do.

Volunteers came from all branches of the British Army. There were Scots, Irish, Welsh, English and New Zealanders.

Bushmills Presbyterian Church

Once the board had made their final selection, training commenced. Although based at Weymouth in Dorset the Commando trained all over the British Isles. Eventually a Commando Training School was established at Achnacarry near Fort William in Scotland. Both the Scottish and Welsh countryside provided the mountains, cliffs ,rivers and lakes that allowed the Commandos to perfect their skills These were the forerunners of the Special Air Service and Special Boat Service. Commandos were recruited into the Special Operations Executive to become agents within occupied countries.

The Commando learned to navigate in unfamiliar water in the dark and to wade ashore silently whilst laden with equipment. They also learned how to use the famous commando-fighting knife; a knife specially designed by a Norwegian and manufactured by Wilkinson, the razor people.

Being pressed by me, John (J.E.D.) Price produced his fighting knife. It is a beautifully crafted weapon. Perfectly balanced it sat comfortably in my hand and even though the knife was almost sixty years old it was still as sharp as a razor.

Those among the volunteers who didn't make the grade were R.T.U. (returned to unit) likewise if they received any major injury during training.

Joe was picked for "G" troop NO 4 Commando. The letter was later changed to"B" Troop. Here he met Chris Birmingham of the 2nd Battalion, Royal Ulster Rifles, a fellow Irishman.

No 4 Commando was based at Troon, Ayrshire, Scotland.

On arrival at Ayr in Scotland, NO. 4 Commando re-grouped at Churchill Barracks. Pausing only long enough for a photograph. NO 4 marched off. With bayonets fixed they marched via Prestwick and Monkton to arrive at Troon.

In Troon the Commandos were allocated civilian billets. Joe and several others were given comfortable digs in the harbour area of Troon.

Every day "B" Troop had to assemble at McLean's coalyard in Union Street for inspection and training. Sunday was always considered an easy day. It consisted of only one forced march in full kit. The march went from Troon to Maybole with a ten-minute break at Maybole. A round trip of approximately 65 miles.

No. 3 Memorial

My mother lived with her parents and family at 15 Union Street, Troon. Union Street is a cul-de-sac. No 15 was at the bottom of the cul-de-sac. McLeans coalyard was about half way down.

The first time that mum met Joe she was not at all impressed. She thought him to be cocky and forward.

He and another Commando were standing at the entrance to Union Street when my mother and her pal were returning home from work. The two Commandos started to chat them up as they passed, and had the cheek to follow them down and ask for a date. When Mum got home she told her mother and sisters about the cheeky Commandos.

A few nights later as mum was returning from work she was met by a solitary Commando at the top of Union Street. He was apologetic but persistent. He was good looking, had a beautiful lilting Irish accent and a wonderful way with words. Eventually mum agreed to a date. Their first date was a night at the pictures. After that their dates were as many as the war would allow. They would often walk out Bentinck Drive, along the tree lined pathway of Craigend Road, up the Isle o' Pin Road and into Fullarton woods. My Dad was gifted with a soft tenor voice and would often sing to her. Her favourite songs were "The Rose of Tralee" and "I'll Walk Beside You". Mum remembers him as the most romantic man in the world.

The relationship between Joseph Watters and Jane McLean Swankie progressed and on the third day of September 1941, they were married in Troon.

Dad would be away for several days at a time. Mum never knew if he was on a raid or off training in some picturesque part of Scotland. Naturally, the Commando were never allowed to tell.

Between 4th march 1941 and august 19th 1942, the Commandos carried out raids on;

Lofoten Islands, Bardia, Crete, Litani River, Tobruk, Rommels H.Q., Vaagso, ST Nazaire and DIEPPE were may father was killed.

My Mum did say that every time Dad came home it was like another honeymoon. This resulted in my birth on the 11th August, 1942.

When Mum fell pregnant she and Dad were living in rooms in Kennedy Road, Troon. They decided that it would be better to move in with

Grannie Swankie in Union Street until after I was born. Dad thoroughly enjoyed his time there and wrote a letter to his sister Martha in Belfast saying how comfortable Grannie had made them.

During their married life Mum and Dad managed a few brief holidays in Belfast and Bushmills with Dads family. Mum adored his family and loved Bushmills, a sentiment that I share today.

My quest to learn more about my father and the circumstances of his death have lead me to read many books and publications dealing with the Commando in general and NO 4s participation in the Dieppe Raid in particular.

THE DIEPPE RAID, 19th AUGUST, 1942

In 1942 German forces occupied most of Europe including Normandy, Northern France. The town of Dieppe was heavily fortified. Two gun batteries each consisting six, six inch guns were placed one to the West and one to the East. The guns were directed out to sea both as a defensive measure and a means of destroying allied convoys. A large number of Canadian assault troops assisted by 50 U.S. rangers were to attack and secure Dieppe. First the gun batteries had to be destroyed. NO 4 Commandos task was to destroy the Hess battery Varengeville Sur-Mer three and a half miles west of Dieppe.

They went in dark splitting into two groups when they landed. Troops “A” and “C” with support were to engage the enemy in a frontal assault having reached the top of the cliffs. Troops “B” (JOE) and “F” led by Lt. Col. The Lord Lovat would land on the beach at Varengeville at the mouth of the river Saane. From the beach Troops “B” and “F” moved up the east bank of the river Saane one thousand yards inland. They then turned east and moved 1900 yards bringing them to wood behind Hess gun battery.

The NO. 4 Commando raid was a complete success.

Out of the 250 Commandos involved only nine were killed unfortunately, one of them was my father.

German losses at the Hess battery were 32 dead, 20 wounded, 4 prisoners. The remainder retreated south.

In his report of Friday 21st August 1942. Lt. Col. The Lord Lovat praised his Commandos and the Royal Navy.

Lance Corporal George Scanlon, a trained medic and Commando saw my father fall. He knew that nothing could be done for him but lifted his body out of the way of further harm.

Until recently I was under the impression that this was my fathers final resting place.

I am now in the possession of a copy of a letter written by a Monsieur Cadot who as fourteen-year-old boy living on the estate where the Hess battery was sited, witnessed the entire raid.

Toward the end of his letter he states that, after the raid was over, a Monsieur Govel collected the dead Commandos in a cart, took them to nearby Sainte-Marguerite and buried them in a cemetery there. Monsieur

Cadot now lives near Prouville not far from Dieppe.

The Commandos were disbanded in 1946. They then formed "The old comrades Association of Army Commandos " This was shortened to "The Commando Association"

Many of the No.4 Commandos remained in Troon after the war marrying local girls. In Chris Birmingham's words,

"The Germans couldn't capture us, but the lassies in Troon could".

RIFLEMAN JOSEPH WATTERS COMMEMORATED ON BROOKWOOD MEMORIAL TO THE MISSING. PANEL 14 COLUMN 3

A Tribute To The 4th Commando

For Their Part In The Dieppe
Raid August 1942

OH, gallant men our nations pride
Whose valour cannot be denied
Their name is echoed far and wide
The Fighting Fourth Commando.

Their deeds shall live from age to age
They've writ their name on History's page
Upheld their glorious heritage
The Fighting Fourth Commando.

At dawn they made that fateful raid
Advancing grim and undismayed
They fought undaunted,unafraid
The Fighting Fourth Commando.

For us they trod the depths of hell
Faced certain death from fire and shell
They did their job,they did it well
The Fighting Fourth Commando.

Some paid the price with battle scars
Some passed beyond all earthly bars
Their names are written in the stars
The Fighting Fourth Commando

Oh,Lord above,who art with us yet
When Time her healing hand hath set
Be with us Lord "Lest we forget"
The Gallant Fourth Commando.

KILLED IN ACTION.

The War Office has intimated to Mrs. Joseph Watters that her husband was killed in the Dieppe raid. This gallant young soldier, who is the elder son of Mr. and Mrs. James Watters, Bushmills, served in China for six years. He had short leave home about 18 months ago, and afterwards served with the Commandos. About four weeks ago he visited his father and mother in Bushmills. Much sympathy is felt for his young wife and their two weeks old child.

WATTERS—In everlasting memory of my darling husband, Joseph Watters, Royal Ulster Rifles, killed August, 1942.

I still hear your laughter,
I whisper your name;
This world, dear, without you,
Will never be the same.

Always remembered by his loving wife and wee son, Jim.—15 Union Street, Troon, Ayrshire, Scotland.

WATTERS—In fond remembrance of Private Joseph Watters, Royal Ulster Rifles, who was killed in action, August, 1942.

His warfare is over, his battle fought,
His victory won though dearly bought;
His fresh young life he gladly gave,
He slumbers now in a hero's grave.

Thought land and sea divide the spot
Where he is gently sleeping,
Still in our hearts he is not forgot,
But in our Saviour's keeping.

Ever remembered by his father, mother, sisters and brother—Upper Main Street, Bushmills.

WATTERS—In sad and loving memory of my dear brother, Joe, Royal Ulster Rifles, killed August, 1942.

Not just to-day but every day I
remember.

Remembered always by his sister, M. Holmes and three little nephews, Robin, Ian and Barrie—The Bungalow, Upper Malone Road, Belfast.

KILLED IN ACTION.

WATTERS—August, 1942, killed in action at Dieppe, Joseph (Commandos), elder son of Mr. and Mrs. James Watters, Upper Main Street, Bushmills.

Thy purpose, Lord, we cannot see,
For all is well that is done by Thee.

Deeply regretted by his mother, father, brother and sisters.

REMEMBERANCE

THEY REMEMBER THEIR COMRADES
THOSE WHO FOUGHT AND FELL,
BUT THOSE THAT REMEMBER THEIR COMRADES
ALSO WENT THROUGH HELL.

LET US ALL REMEMBER THE FALLEN
AND I HAVE LOST ONE SO DEAR,
BUT LET US NEVER FORGET THE SURVIVORS
THOSE WHO LIVED WITH FEAR.

THOSE WHO SHALL LIVE WITH THE MEMORIES
OF HORROR AND OF PAIN,
OF SADNESS AND OF SUFFERING
THAT THEY NEVER WANT TO SEE AGAIN.

THEY HAVE PUT ASIDE THE TALKING
AND MANS INHUMANITY TO MAN,
SOME ACCEPT THEIR LOSS OF SIGHT
OR A LEG OR A FOOT OR AN ARM.

SOME ACCEPT OTHER INJURIES
THE ONES THAT CAN'T BE SEEN,
BROUGHT ON BY SHOCK AND REVULSION
OF THE ENEMYS KILLING MACHINE.

LET US REMEMBER THEM ALL
AT THE GOING DOWN OF THE SUN,
THEY ARE ALL OUR HEROS
EVERY
SINGLE
ONE.

JAMES WATTERS
TROON.

IN MEMORY OF HIS FATHER
RIFLEMAN JOSEPH WATTERS FROM BUSHMILLS

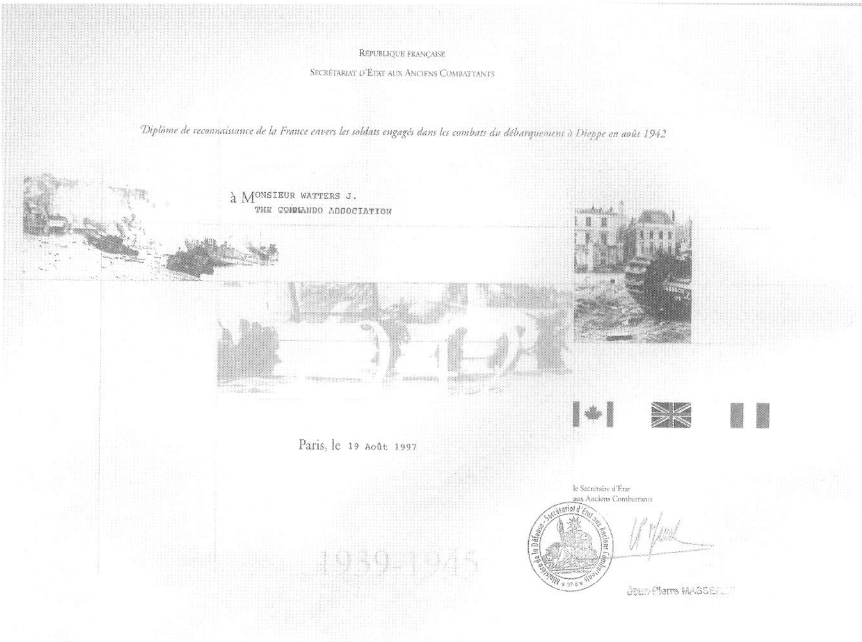

RÉPUBLIQUE FRANÇAISE

SECRÉTARIAT D'ÉTAT AUX ANCIENS COMBATTANTS

Diplôme de reconnaissance de la France envers les soldats engagés dans les combats du débarquement à Dieppe en août 1942

à MONSIEUR WATTERS J.
THE COMMANDO ASSOCIATION

Paris, le 19 Août 1997

1939-1945

le Secrétaire d'État
aux Anciens Combattants

Ministère de la Défense - Secrétariat d'État aux Anciens Combattants

Jean-Pierre MASSERET

Commando Memorial, Spleen Bridge, Scotland

SCOTTISH
THE ROYAL
ULSTER RIFLES
LIEUTENANT
GRENNAN J. M.C.
WARRANT OFFR.III
CLEMENTS J. McM.
SERJEANT
BRYSON M.
CORPORAL
PORTERFIELD G.
RIFLEMAN
HODSON A.
McAREE P.
McCONNELL W.J.
McCOOL F.
MAHON M.
WATTERS J.
THE LONDON
IRISH RIFLES

William Cochrane

Gunner 2049776

390 Bty., 27 Searchlight Regiment, Royal Artillery

Died 4th December, 1942

Age 35

William was the dearly loved second son of James and Elizabeth Cochrane of Dundarave.

DIED OF WOUNDS

It was with deep regret that the people of the town and district heard on Friday of the death of Mr William Cochrane, Dundarave, Bushmills. Educated at Giants Causeway P.E. school and Ballycastle High School. He was appointed to the clerical staff of the British andAmerican Tobacco Co., London. Prior to the outbreak of war, he volunteered for service with the Territorial Army, and when the war broke out he joined a Searchlight Regiment of the Royal Artillery.

The sad news of his death from wounds in the Middle East was conveyed to his parents. They had ironically received a letter from William on the same day, stating that he was well and hoped the family would have a happy reunion at Christmas 1943. Two other brothers, Dan and James are serving with the 8th Army in the Middle East.

COLERAINE CHRONICLE

Mr. William Cochrane, son of Mr. James Cochrane and Mrs. Cochrane, Dundarave, Bushmills, died of wounds in the Middle East. December, 1942.

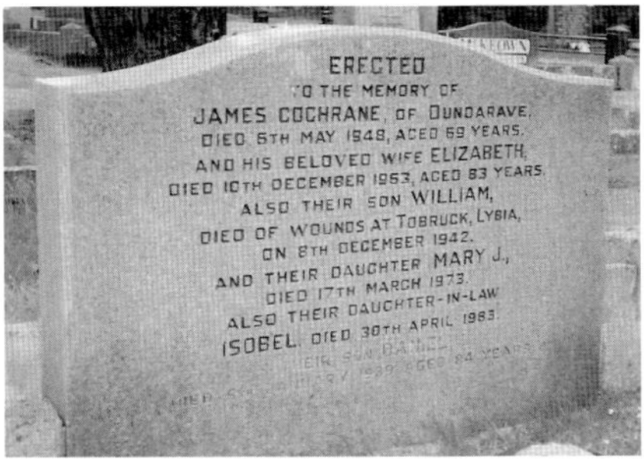

WILLIAM COCHRANE

Williams unit had gone to Tubruk on 16th November and they were deployed around the harbour in an A.A. defensive role. A number of enemy aircraft had attacked the area, in some instances two aircraft attacks were made, one going inland and the other attacking the harbour. Search lights engaged the enemy and strong evasive action was taken.

One Junkers 88 was illuminated by the detachment at lite C2. This aircraft while illuminated climbed slowly, then steeply, cranked to the right, dived and started to climb again, rolled over to the right, turned and dived into the ground.

During this action a considerable number of H.E.bombs were dropped, one of which fell on the H.Q. killing and wounding. Slight damage was done to the projector but it was repaired and the site was in action again 90 minutes after the raid.

William is commemorated on Dunluce Parish Memorial and is buried in Tobruk, Libya, Section 1 Row a Grave 6

TOBRUK WAR CEMETERY, LIBYA

Tubruk is a sea port on the Mediterranean coast with an excellent deep water harbour.

During the second world war it was important to the allies and the enemy, for the reception of supplies and reinforcements.

Tubruk Commonwealth Cemetery lies inland and contains nearly 2,500 war graves.

Many soldiers from the 8th army involved in the desert campaign are buried here.

27 (London Electrical Engineers) SL Regt RA(TA)

Locations

Aug 40	Formed from 27 AA Bn RE	
Aug 40	47 AA Bde	Southampton, UK
Jul 41	British Troops Egypt	N Africa
Nov 41	Middle East Forces	N Africa
Jun 45	Suspended animation	

Batteries

Sep 41 304, 305, 306, 390

Notes

May 41 - 304 Bty in Crete
Late 41 - 2 Troops 306 Bty at Tobruk & 2 Troops 390 Bty at Alexandria

Tobruk Cemetery, Libya

Samuel Morton

Stoker 1st Class
D/KK 132552

H.M. Tug St, Royal Navy

Died 28th December, 1942

Age 31

Samuel was the son of Robert and Elizabeth Morton of Ballytober, Priestland. He was also their third son to be killed in action. His brother John being killed in WW1 and Albert killed later in 1944.

> It was with feelings of profound sadness that the news was heard of the death on active service of Stoker Samuel Morton, Ballytober.
>
> A young man in the prime of his life, he joined the Royal Navy in 1941. The Morton family have resided at Priestland and Ballytober for at least four generations and are held in high esteem.
>
> Samuel leaves a young wife who resides in England.

COLERANE CHRONICLE DECEMBER, 1942

H.M. tug St. was torpedoed at Benghazi.

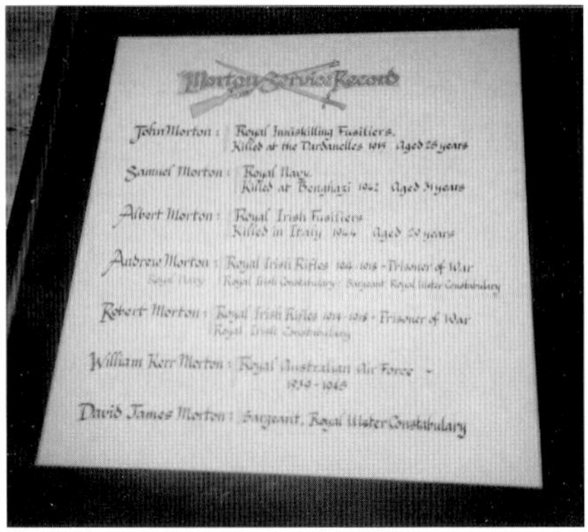

Samuel is commemorated on Dunluce Parish Memorial and Plymouth Naval Memorial Panel 70 Column 2.

There are 7000 sailors from the Great War and 16000 from the second world war commemorated here.

Charges to pay
s. d.
RECEIVED
POST OFFICE
TELEGRAM
No. 4
OFFICE STAMP
PRIESTLAND
3 JA 43
Prefix. Time handed in. Office of Origin and Service Instructions. Words.
9-50 m
55 London T. 11
From
To
Samuel missing Presumed Killed. writing Nellie Morton
For free repetition of doubtful words telephone "TELEGRAMS ENQUIRY" or call, with this form at office of delivery. Other enquiries should be acc[illegible] by this form and if possible, the envelope
B or C

William John Tweed

Fusilier 6979743

1st Bn., Royal Irish Fusiliers

Died 19th January, 1943

Age 20

William John Tweed died of wounds received from the enemy at Tobruk.

The 1st battalion of the Royal Irish Fusiliers first went to North Africa in November 1942 as part of Operation Torch, designed to defeat the axis forces there.

In January they found themselves fighting in Tunisia. They moved forward from Duvat to El Aroussa and on the 16th reached an area known as Hill 329. The Germans were in a strong position there. This was reconnoitred and on the 19th an attack went forward against the position.

The 1st Bn. of the R.I.F. were concentrating on moving forward to their objective of infiltrating the enemy, on arrival they saw no signs of the enemy, so they shelled known areas.

Still no movement was seen, so they moved down being covered by their own men and special weapons, they searched the area and found that a party of perhaps about 30 strong had been lying in a heavily concealed ambush for several days, main equipment including mines. They had left in a hurry as a great quantity of stores and weapons had been left behind and from the amount of blood left in the ground, it was definite that the casualties had been large and serious. They then withdrew at dusk.

The stretcher bearers had been given permission to go back to the battlefield to recover the bodies of Major Murphy and Captain Barstow. This they were allowed to do if the 6th Inniskillings could provide cover. They were unable to do this due to commitments of their own, but the stretcher bearers pushed out on their own. They returned later not having found the bodies, believing that it was because they were not able to penetrate deep enough. They tried once more and went further. They could see the enemies head and shoulders above their slit trenches, watching them as they searched for the bodies. The Germans did not fire on them when they were carrying the stretchers, but opened fire when they put them down.

William was obviously wounded during this battle, and later died of his wounds.

William was the only son of Mary Nicholl of 1 Ballyness East Bushmills. He is commemorated on Dunluce Parish Memorial, Medjez-el-Bab War Cemetery Tunisia Section 8 Row E Grave 9.

2903 identified graves

387 unidentified

A Standard Bearer of the Royal British Legion paying tribute to William Tweed.

William Kerr

Gunner 6980756

1/1 Maritime Regt., Royal Artillery

Died Wednesday, 24th February 1943

Age 22

William formerly lived at Dunseverick but his parents John and Alice Kerr moved to Ballyrock.

Before joining the army William was employed by Mr. T. McCandless, Portrush, as a bricklayer.

William was posted as missing in action on the 24th of February. His parents were officially notified that he had indeed lost his life at sea on that date.

William was the youngest son and his brother Martin served with the Royal Engineers in Italy. His sister Tilly was married to John Elliott of Turfahun.

Gunner William Kerr, Royal Artillery (Light A.A.), youngest son of Mr. and Mrs. J. Kerr, Ballyrock, Bushmills, reported missing since February, 1943, now presumed killed in action at sea.

We little thought when he left home
That he would never return
That he so soon would sleep
In an unknown soldiers grave.

Deeply missed by his father, mother, brothers and sisters.

Commemorated on Portsmouth Naval Memorial Panel 80 Column 3, in honour of the Navy and to the abiding memory of these Ranks and Ratings of this port who laid down their lives and have no other grave than the sea

William is also commemorated on Dunseverick Church Memorial and Billy Parish Church.

John Kerr married Alice McConaghie

- **John married Maggie McVicker**
  - William
  - Harold
  - Ivan
  - Margaret
- **Andy married Nellie McKendry**
- **Martin married Katy Brown**
  - Lex
  - Jackie
- **WILLIAM Killed in Action**
- **Tillie married John Elliott**
  - Violet
  - Jean
  - John
  - May
  - Irene
  - Jim
  - Anne
- **Mary married John Mckay**
  - Mary
  - Margaret
- **Letty Married Tom Ginty**
  - John
  - Maria

James Macready

Sergeant
1037956
W.Op./ Air Gunner

221 Sqd. Royal Air Force Volunteer Reserve

Died 2nd February, 1944

Age 21

James Andrew Macready was the only son of James and Violet Macready of Ballyliken, Bushmills. His father James served for many years on Ballymoney Rural District Council. He had two sisters Anna and Jean, Anna was employed at Ballyrashane Creamery and Jean was a nurse in Belfast.

James was educated at Ballytober P.E.S. and Bushmills Secondary School. He joined the R.A.F. in 1924 at the age of twenty and served overseas for a year.

His sister received a letter from James which was delivered to her, two days after the telegram to say that he had been killed in action.

James joined the R.A.F with William Rankin of Ballylough. At a service in Dunluce Presbyterian Church, the Minister, Rev. Alexander made a sympathetic reference to James. He referred to him as still a teenager, he had heard and nobly responded to the call of King and Country. He had not chosen an easy or safe place, but had undertaken an arduous and dangerous duty. His service to the cause of liberty had been entirely free and spontaneous. They had known him as a boy and young man in their midst, and as such they would ever remember him.

There was no serious fighting near the town of Bari, which was the army

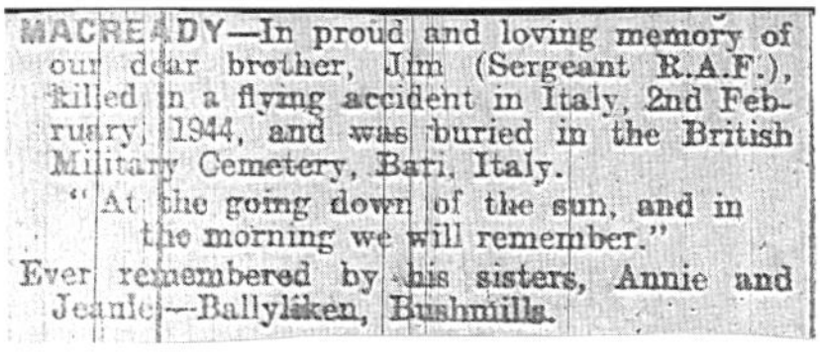

MACREADY—In proud and loving memory of our dear brother, Jim (Sergeant R.A.F.), killed in a flying accident in Italy, 2nd February, 1944, and was buried in the British Military Cemetery, Bari, Italy.

"At the going down of the sun, and in the morning we will remember."

Ever remembered by his sisters, Annie and Jeanie—Ballyliken, Bushmills.

headquarters during the early stages of the Italian Campaign, but it continued to be an important supply base and the 98th general hospital was based there until the end of the war. James Macready was killed in a flying accident while stationed here

At the going down of the sun
And in the morning
We will remember

Ever remembered by his sisters
Annie and Jeanie, Ballyliken.

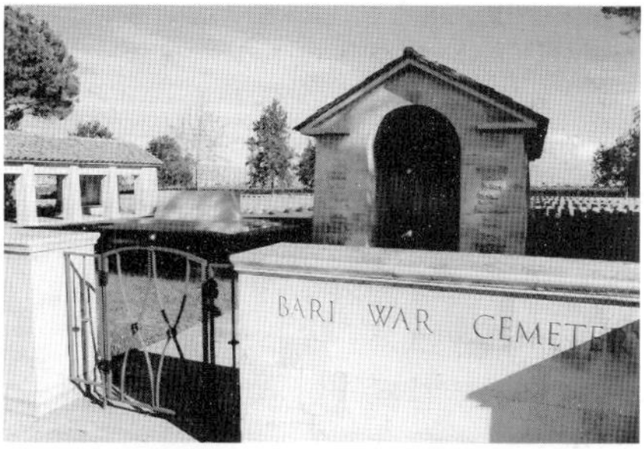

Commemorated on his family headstone in Dunluce Presbyterian Church and on Church Memorial.

James is buried in Bari war cemetery, Italy.

There are 2128 burials from the Second World War in this Cemetery.

No 221 Squadron

RNAS Unit in the Aegean, were allocated RAF squadron numbers but it would seem that these numbers did not really begin to be used until September, by which time movement and amalgamation of the original units led to some confusion. The number 221 was originally allocated to 'D' Squadron of no 2 Wing RNAS at Stavros, which was composed of anti-submarine flights of seaplanes. However, by the time the number 221 was brought into use, the squadron was equipped with DH9 day bombers and at the same time was sub-divided into Nos 552, 553 and 554 Flights. In October it moved to Mudros and then in December was despatched to South Russia to assist the 'White' Russians in their fight against the 'Red' Bolsheviks. With the failure of this campaign, the squadron disbanded on 1 September 1919.

The squadron reformed on 21 November 1940 as a general reconnaissance unit at Bircham Newton equipped with Wellingtons. Operations in the form of convoy escorts began in February 1941 and anti-shipping operations began in March but in May the squadron it transferred to Limavady in Northern Ireland, where it began anti-submarine patrols. In September it moved once again, this time to Iceland, returning to Docking at the end of the year.

At the beginning of 1942, it was in transit, again, this time to the Middle East. Until the squadron's ground echelon arrived its aircraft and crews operated with No 47 Squadron. From March 1942 until March 1943 the squadron operated from bases in North Africa, conducting anti-submarine patrols, shipping reconnaissance missions and shipping strikes. During this period it began using Leigh Lights to carry out nights attacks against shipping and submarines and specialised in night torpedo attacks. However, from May 1943, the quantity of targets declined and it began to bomb enemy ports but by September 1943 even this had ended and the squadron was mainly involved in anti-submarine patrols. Moving to Italy in March 1944, it resumed its strike role against shipping in the Adriatic, which it continued on moving to Greece in October.

With the end of the war in sight, the squadron returned to Egypt in April 1945, disbanding at Idku on 25 August.

James Andrew McCaughan

Sergeant 5506096

Hampshire Regiment and No. 3 Commando

Died Tuesday 22nd February, 1944

James Andrew McCaughan was born on the 28th March 1916 in Ballynock, Castlequarter, Ballymoney. Castlequarter is a townland about ten miles east of Ballymoney town, alongside there are two further townlands called Ballynock little and Ballynock big. These are divided by the Pharis Road leading from Ballymoney. Ballynock is north of Ballymoney in Ballyrashane Parish.

According to his birth certificate his parents were James McCaughan a soldier, and Jane McCaughan nee McFahey (possibly Fahey). No trace of Jane has yet been found.

No. 3 Commando Memorial at National Arboretum, Staffordshire

Dunluce Parish Church

James Andrew had a sister Sadie, she is believed to have been older than James and resided in Bushmills, and became Sadie Nicholl of Ballyness.

In James Andrews service record, he lists his home town as Bushmills. He lists his date of birth as 28th March, 1914, he intended to join up two years before his legal entry date.

It appears he served with the 2nd Cameronians for three years. This Regiment was stationed at Bordon Camp near Headley Hampshire in England. It was while he was stationed there, he met my grandmother Doris Lilian White. Doris lived with her parents Arthur William and Florence White at Shingle Cottage Beach, Hill Road Headley.

They were married on the 7th December, 1935, James Andrew was twenty one as was Doris Lillian. He lists his name as Andrew, as Doris referred to him as "Big Andy" in later years. I can only assume this was because his fathers name was also James. They both signed the marriage certificate in the presence of Arthur White, Doris' father and also her brother Arthur White junior.

He left the army and for a while worked for Chapman Lowry and

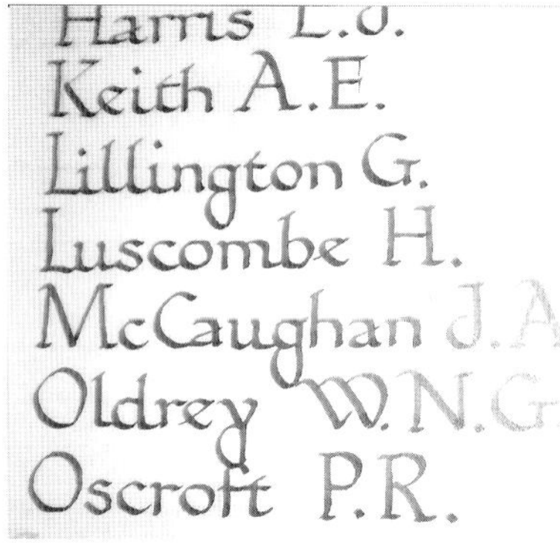

Roll of Honour, Anglican Church, Rangoon, Burma

Puttick, a builders based in Haselmere, near Hindhead, Surrey.

James Andrew and Doris had one son. William Andrew (named after Arthur William his grandfather and Andrew his father).

William Andrew was born on 7th April 1936 at Shingle Cottage in Headley.

James Andrew is recorded with his occupation being a labourer. Living at Shingle Cottage now were Arthur and Florence, James Andrew(known as big Andy) Doris and baby William, who they decided to call little Andy.

James Andrew either joined or was called up on 20th June, 1940. He joined the Hampshire Regiment. This regiment was based at Parkhurst Prison on the isle of Wight. In November 1940 James attended the Hythe Wing small arms school, and qualified, but was also wounded. In October 1942 after few scraps and being court marshalled, he regained

GVI RI

HONI SOIT QUI MAL Y PENSE

DIEU ET MON DROIT

This scroll commemorates

Serjeant James MCCAUGHAN

The Hampshire Regt

held in honour as one who served King and Country in the world war of 1939-1945 and gave his life to save mankind from tyranny. May his sacrifice help to bring the peace and freedom for which he died.

his rank of sergeant and attended a S.A.S M.T. course and in September-October 1943 he qualified as an Arms Instructor.

James seemed to be a bit of a nomad with a wandering streak. He volunteered for attachment to No. 3 Commando in 1942. Then back again to the Hampshire Regiment in 1943. He then volunteered for posting to Nigeria, West Africa and served there with the 8th Battalion the Gold Coast Regiment, in May-August 1943.

He then left Nigeria for India in August 1943, he was taken on by the India Command 2nd Echelon (G.H.Q.) and attended a weapons training refresher course.

This regiment was sent to Ngakyedauk pass (known as Okedoke pass) in the defence of a village called Sinzweka. The Burma star association have the story of Njakyedauk box on their web site.

The following story is taken from there.

There wee several bloody battles fought there, in torrential rain-the report says "the rain poured down upon this jungle and its narrow tracks. The mud deepened, the branches dripped in melancholy rhythm and progress towards the box, slowed down most seriously. Jeeps skidded into streams, heavier trucks became embedded in the mire and blocked the way through the scrub oaks and undergrowth. Nobody knew what had

happened and many knew nothing apart from their orders to move to a given point.

Anxious and confused, men slithered on the slopes, sweated and swore as they struggled, to drag their frightened, obstinate mules and equipment up hill. So slippery was the muddy surface of the tracks that when the mule loads had been taken off the saddles and laid in the slush, the mules still stumbled and kicked in their game efforts to mount the slope.

Drivers of jeeps and ambulances decided to wait until they were obliged to move on, without skidding into a bank.

The tanks were unable to go out from

the mud, and had the sun not shone mercifully that afternoon to dry up the tracks, the situation might have deteriorated to a most grievous extent. At the end of the pass it was a grim scene that met the troops.

Troops hanging around waiting for someone to tell them what to do, and others in from Messervys Headquarters that was now in Japanese hands. There was an air of bewilderment, fear and relief and hope of escaping alive.

There were lots of attacks by the Japanese on this box, wanting the stores, ammunition and food, and at one time split the box in half, separating several regiments, including the Ghurkhas and Indians fleeing into the jungle.

Day after day those who defended the box turned their eyes northwards when, their ears caught the drone of approaching aircraft above the noise of the shells and bullets, tank engines, and men's shouts and the clattering of mules beneath the trees. Through the hatch doors, were pushed boxes of ammunition of many sizes, petrol, bales of equipment, rations, and countless items that could protect, feed and hearten the garrison below.

Fodder for the animals and batteries, telephones, cable all these and more came drifting down towards the paddy fields, in a host of white parachutes.

The advance started on the 12th February 1944 and the early hours of the 14 were marked by a severe blow, and their hopes of early relief were dashed. During the night some 200

Taukkyan War Cemetery

Japanese soldiers continuously attacked the positions, their onslaught from the east and west was made, regardless of the cost. This was a serious setback. General Biggs ordered 123 Brigade to take every reasonable risk to re-open the pass, at the earliest possible moment.

Many of the troops were weakened by malaria and dysentery and the evacuation of casualties totalled no less than 478. Night after night

the Japanese flung themselves at our defences, at any moment a shell might land in our part of the box. So crowded was the area that few shells didn't strike man or mule, ammunition or petrol store, tank or jeep or tent or shelter.

An hour before first light on the 21st February 70 Japanese soldiers marched down the road, through the eastern gate of the box. They moved in formation and were savaged by the Ghurkhas and by the 25th Dragoons. 42 enemy corpses were counted on the ground when daylight came. Also on the 21st February the troops attacked and the final opening of the Pass was now in sight. Every known Japanese position had been pounded by the R.A.F. Now the only hill to be cleared was the dominating sugar loaf that overlooked the box. When sugar loaf was reached the siege of Ngakyedauk was at an end. It was here that on the 22nd february, 1944 that James Andrew lost his life.

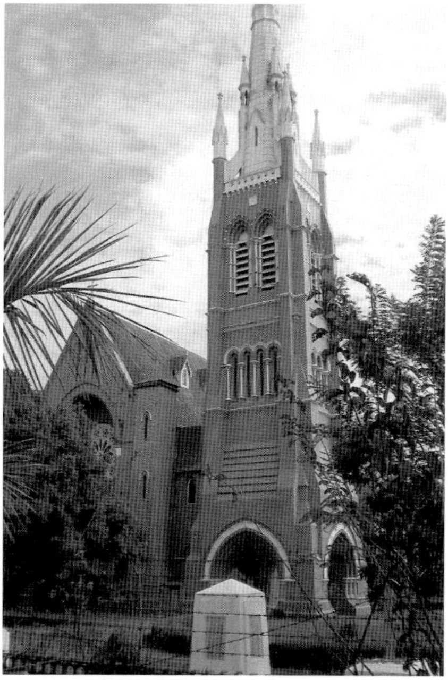

Rangoon Anglican Church

Ironic that at the very end when victory was in sight that this was the battle that saw many men killed in action and James was just one of them.

He was buried with military honours in India. When the commonwealth war graves commission was set up to honour and look after the graves of the deceased soldiers, it was decided to have a main cemetery in Rangoon, now know as Taukkyan war cemetery.

Men that were killed in India were relocated into one corner of the Cemetery, and James Andrew is buried there.

His inscription reads

"In memory of Sergeant James Andrew McCaughan 5506096., And no.3 commando who died aged 29 on Tuesday 22nd February, 1944. Sergeant McCaughan, husband of Doris Lilian McCaughan of Headley Hampshire. Remembered with Honour"

His inscription is also recorded in Rangoon church, Headley Church and War Memorial, Bushmills War Memorial and Dunluce Parish Church.

The Petersfield and district post records the death of James Andrew:

"Killed in action- well known and popular in Headley, where he had lived for a good many years, the death has been confirmed of Sergeant James Andrew McCaughan, who had been serving with the Commandos. He was killed in action.

Sergeant McCaughan was a regular soldier before the war. His wife, Mrs Doris McCaughan, who is left with a young son, is a daughter of Arthur and Florence White, of shingle cottage Headley."

Doris remained in the house with her mother and father for the rest of her life. She eventually remarried Samuel Ellison, and he became a good father to William Andrew.

William married twice, having two children, Susan Lilian in February 1963 and Ian Andrew in July 1966.

Susan has been researching her grandfather for nearly thirty years and has provided this story and photographs of her grandfather.

There are 6374 burials in this cemetery.

James Andrew with his wife Doris and son Andrew

James Andrew serving in 2nd Cameronians

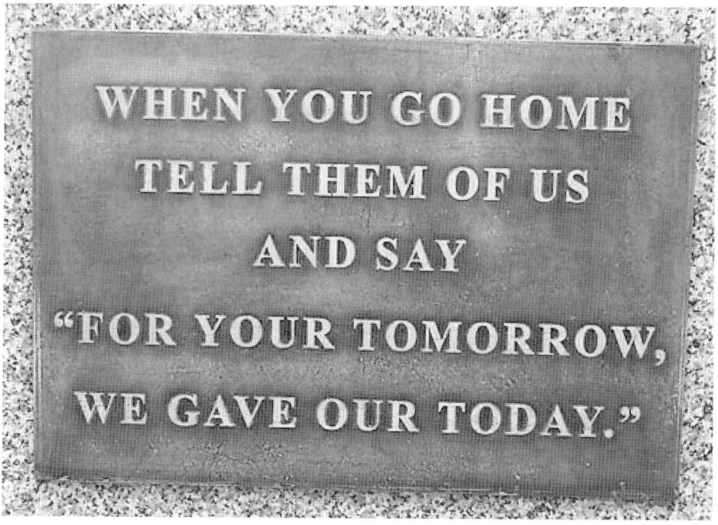

Memorial to all Allied Forces

William Black Rankin

Sergeant Air Gunner
1795202

166 Sqd., Royal Air Force Volunteer Reserve

Died 22nd May, 1944

William Rankin was the 20 year old son of Mr and Mrs Matt Rankin of Ballyclough, Bushmills. He was educated at Ballytober P.E. School and Bushmills Secondary School.

William received an outstanding reference from his Headmaster Mr. R.C. Salisbury, and this enabled him to join the Royal Air Force. He had been a member of the school air training corps where he held the rank of sergeant. He also was an outstanding hockey player, and interested in all out of school activities. He passed with credits in history, geography and english.

On 28th May 1944 Mr and Mrs Rankin received a telegram to say that their son was reported missing as a result of air operations on the night of 21/22 May 1944.

A letter from wing commander D.A. Garner of Kirmington Lincolnshire stated that the aircraft was missing and that their son may be a Prisoner of War. This was the first of many letters that the family was to receive from the R.A.F. Mr and Mrs Rankin were determined to find out what happened to their son and never gave up hope that he might return.

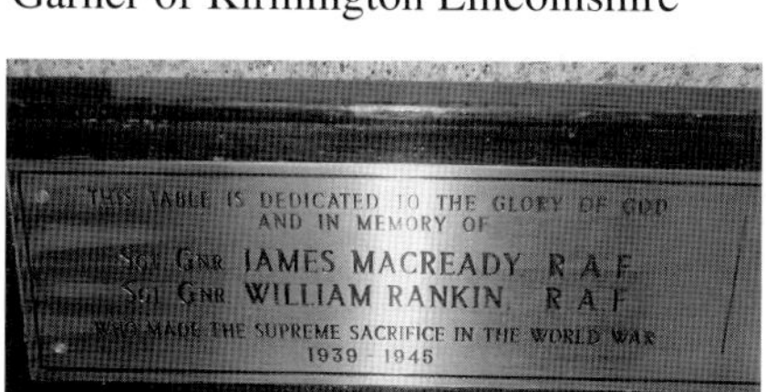

Dunluce Presbyterian Church Memorial

The Lancaster in which William was a mid-upper gunner failed to return from a bombing raid on Duisburg. The ministry was working with the international red cross committee to try and find out if William was indeed a Prisoner of War.

18th July the family were informed that on that date the Pilot Officer had been captured and the other officers had lost their lives. This information came from german documents.

By 26th May, 1949 Mr. Rankin had

been informed officially that his son had indeed lost his life on 2nd June, 1944. The search officers had ascertained that his body had been washed ashore at Scheveningen, near the Hague in Holland. The Germans had buried him in an unknown grave in Westduin Cemetery. By means of captured German documents they were able to identify him to correspondence found on his person at the time of the burial.

Two of the crew survived. P/O J.W. Reilley and F/O Pochailo R.C.A.F.

William Black Rankin Wesduin Cemetery the Hague, Holland

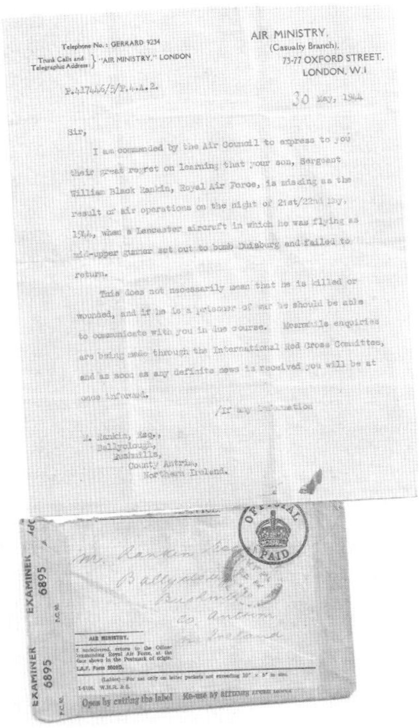
Telephone No.: GERRARD 9234
Trunk Calls and Telegraphic Address: "AIR MINISTRY," LONDON

AIR MINISTRY,
(Casualty Branch),
73-77 OXFORD STREET,
LONDON, W.1

P.417446/5/P.4.A.2.

30 May, 1944

Sir,

I am commanded by the Air Council to express to you their great regret on learning that your son, Sergeant William Black Rankin, Royal Air Force, is missing as the result of air operations on the night of 21st/22nd May, 1944, when a Lancaster aircraft in which he was flying as mid-upper gunner set out to bomb Duisburg and failed to return.

This does not necessarily mean that he is killed or wounded, and if he is a prisoner of war he should be able to communicate with you in due course. Meanwhile enquiries are being made through the International Red Cross Committee, and as soon as any definite news is received you will be at once informed.

/If any information

M. Rankin, Esq.,
Ballyclough,
Bushmills,
County Antrim,
Northern Ireland.

The Under-Secretary of State for Air presents his compliments and by Command of the Air Council has the honour to transmit the enclosed Awards granted for service in the war of 1939-45.

The Council share your sorrow that

SERGEANT W.B. RANKIN

in respect of whose service these Awards are granted did not live to receive them.

Reading the correspondence you can get a feel of how desperate the Rankin's were to find out about William as were many families who did not know if their son was still alive as a Prisoner of War or was missing in action never to be traced.

Joan serving in the W.A.A.F. at Upavon in Marlborough knew William, and wrote a distressing letter to Williams mother, stating how worried she was about him as the air ministry had returned all the letters that she had sent him.

John Mostaert from the Hague wrote to Mr and Mrs Rankin in 1964. He sent them a photograph of his daughter and friend at Williams grave.

"They carry flowers for your son,
know that we will never forget what
your son did for us""

William is commemorated on his families grave at Dunluce Presbyterian and on the Church Memorial.

William joined the R.A.F with James Macready of Ballyliken

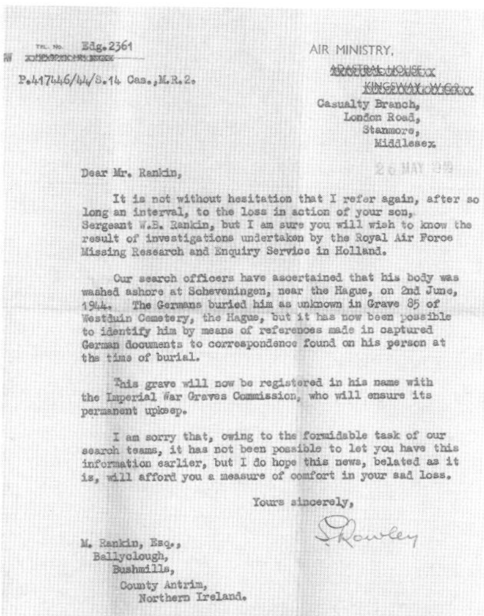

TEL. No. Edg.2361

P.417446/44/S.14 Cas.,M.R.2.

AIR MINISTRY,
~~ADASTRAL HOUSE~~
~~KINGSWAY, W.C.2~~
Casualty Branch,
London Road,
Stanmore,
Middlesex.

2 MAY 9

Dear Mr. Rankin,

It is not without hesitation that I refer again, after so long an interval, to the loss in action of your son, Sergeant W.B. Rankin, but I am sure you will wish to know the result of investigations undertaken by the Royal Air Force Missing Research and Enquiry Service in Holland.

Our search officers have ascertained that his body was washed ashore at Scheveningen, near the Hague, on 2nd June, 1944. The Germans buried him as unknown in Grave 85 of Westduin Cemetery, the Hague, but it has now been possible to identify him by means of references made in captured German documents to correspondence found on his person at the time of burial.

This grave will now be registered in his name with the Imperial War Graves Commission, who will ensure its permanent upkeep.

I am sorry that, owing to the formidable task of our search teams, it has not been possible to let you have this information earlier, but I do hope this news, belated as it is, will afford you a measure of comfort in your sad loss.

Yours sincerely,

S Rowley

M. Rankin, Esq.,
Ballyclough,
Bushmills,
County Antrim,
Northern Ireland.

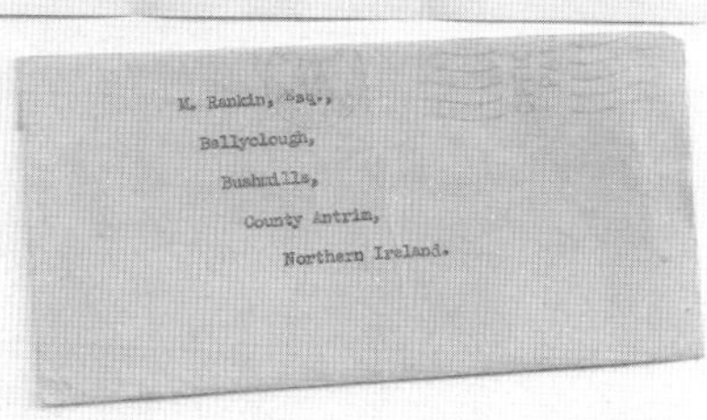

M. Rankin, Esq.,
Ballyclough,
Bushmills,
County Antrim,
Northern Ireland.

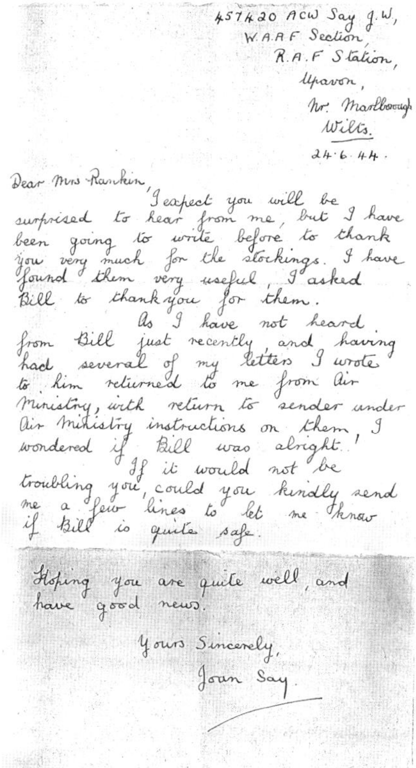

457420 ACW Say J.W,
W.A.A.F Section,
R.A.F Station,
Upavon,
Nr. Marlborough
Wilts.

24.6.44.

Dear Mrs Rankin,

I expect you will be surprised to hear from me, but I have been going to write before to thank you very much for the stockings. I have found them very useful, I asked Bill to thank you for them.

As I have not heard from Bill just recently, and having had several of my letters I wrote to him returned to me from Air Ministry, with return to sender under Air Ministry instructions on them, I wondered if Bill was alright.

If it would not be troubling you, could you kindly send me a few lines to let me know if Bill is quite safe.

Hoping you are quite well, and have good news.

Yours Sincerely,

Joan Say.

THE AIRMAN'S PRAYER

If I climb up to heaven thou art there
If I go down to hell, thou art there also.
If I take the wings of the morning
And remain in the uttermost parts of the sea,
Even there also shall thy hand lead me
And thy right hand shall hold me.

1795202 SERGEANT
W.B. RANKIN
AIR GUNNER
ROYAL AIR FORCE
22ND MAY 1944 AGE 20
REMEMBERED, LOVED
AND LONGED FOR ALWAYS
BY HIS PARENTS AND BROTHERS

KIRMINGTON

This Class A airfield, on which work begun late in 1941, was completed the following summer. Located directly south-west of Kirmington village on the A18 Scunthorpe to Grimsby road, the airfield conformed to the standard of the time with three concrete runways, the main, 04-22, being originally 1,450 yards long, 15-33 1,150 yards, and 09-27 1,100 yards. However, it appears that extension of the runways was carried out before the station was opened and this involved the closure and diversion of the A18 just west of Kirmington village, and also the closure of the minor road running north to the village on the east side of the airfield. When extended the runways lengths were 04-22 at 2,000 yards and the others both 1,400 yards. Of the original 36 pan-type hard standings two were, lost by perimeter track and hangar taxiway extensions. Two loop-type standings were added as replacements. A T2 hangar was located on the main technical site between runway heads 22 and 27 and another on the on a maintenance site near Kirmington Villa with another T2 and a B1 a little to the north. Two blister hangars were erected on pan hard standings adjacent to the technical site T2. The bomb store was off the south side of the airfield and 11 camp sites, of which seven were domestic, were dispersed around Kirmington village and further to the east, allowing for 2,177 males and 345 females.

Kirmington was first used by No. 15 (Pilots) Advanced Flying School from March 1942, but on October 23 that year the station was transferred to No. 1 Group, Bomber Command when No. 150 Squadron and its Wellingtons arrived from Snaith preparatory to having half of its strength despatched to North Africa. The remaining crews continued on operations and were joined in December by part of No. 170 Squadron from Grimsby, which had suffered a similar fate. Instead of re-building both squadrons, a decision was taken by Bomber Command to amalgamate both under another designation. Thus, on January 27, 1943, No. 166 Squadron was re-born, having last existed as a Handley Page V/1500 heavy bomber squadron in the First World War. No.166 flew Wellingtons until September 1943 and then converted to Lancasters. As Bomber Command continued to expand, No.166 lost its C Flight in October 1944 for the re-forming of No. 153 Squadron. It flew its first raid on October 7 but, as was common practice, as soon as the new unit was fully established it was transferred to a station where more room was available. Thus by the middle of the month it had moved to Scampton. During operations from Kirmington, a total 178 bombers either failed to return or were destroyed in crashes, 51 being Wellingtons and 127 Lancasters.

Kirmington continued as home for No. 166 Squadron until November 1945 when, along with several other bomber squadrons, it was disbanded. From February 1946 the station was put on care and maintenance until relinquished by the Air Ministry to the Ministry of Agriculture in 1953. Some private crop spraying and commercial flying with light aircraft took place over the next few years, use being made of wartime buildings by the operators. From summer 1967, a small charter company started regular flying from the airfield and its activities gradually expanded. In 1970 Kirmington was selected as the best location for a regional airport serving the Hull, Grimsby and Scunthorpe localities. By this time the A18 had been restored and took in part of the northern end of runway 22, but the others were in good order although a minor road had been reopened across the flying field. In furtherance of the project, Lindsey County Council purchased the airfield for a reported £85,000, a further £170,000 being invested in refurbishing the runways, building a new terminal and control tower. Opened in March 1974, Kirmington eventually became Humberside Airport and home to small charter airlines. It has since been acquired by Manchester Airport PLC. A memorial plaque to the men of No. 166 Squadron is to be found in Kirmington village church.

R. C. SALISBURY, B.A.
HEADMASTER.

R. JUDGE, SECRETARY,
PORTBALLINTRAE.

THE SECONDARY SCHOOL,
BUSHMILLS,
Co. ANTRIM.

15th October 1941.

William Black Rankin attended this School from September 1938 until June 1941. During that time he worked very well, passing the Junior Certificate of the Ministry of Education for Northern Ireland in 1940, with credits in History and Geography. He sat for the Junior again this year and passed with credits in English, History and Geography.

In addition he played a full part in all out-of-school activities, such as dramatics, athletics and hockey. He has been a member of the School Air Training Corps since its formation early this year and now holds the rank of Sergeant.

I consider that Rankin is a boy of excellent character and that he is very reliable and conscientious.

I have pleasure in giving him a very thorough recommendation.

R. C. Salisbury. B.A. (Hons)
(London).
Headmaster.

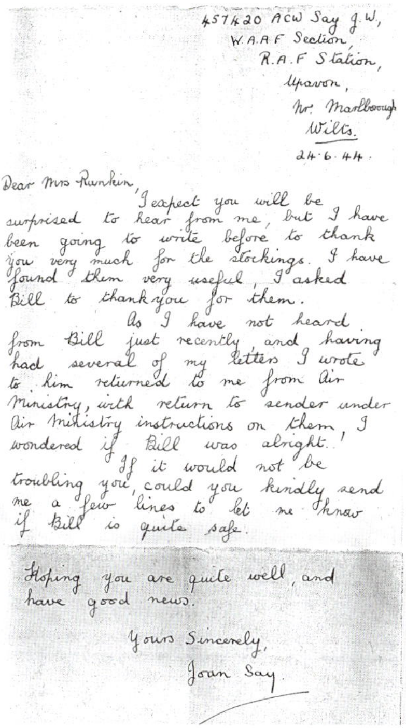

457420 ACW Say J.W,
W.A.A.F Section,
R.A.F Station,
Upavon,
Nr. Marlborough
Wilts.

24·6·44.

Dear Mrs Rankin,

I expect you will be surprised to hear from me, but I have been going to write before to thank you very much for the stockings. I have found them very useful, I asked Bill to thank you for them.

As I have not heard from Bill just recently and having had several of my letters I wrote to him returned to me from Air Ministry, with return to sender under Air Ministry instructions on them, I wondered if Bill was alright.

If it would not be troubling you, could you kindly send me a few lines to let me know if Bill is quite safe.

Hoping you are quite well, and have good news.

Yours Sincerely,

Joan Say.

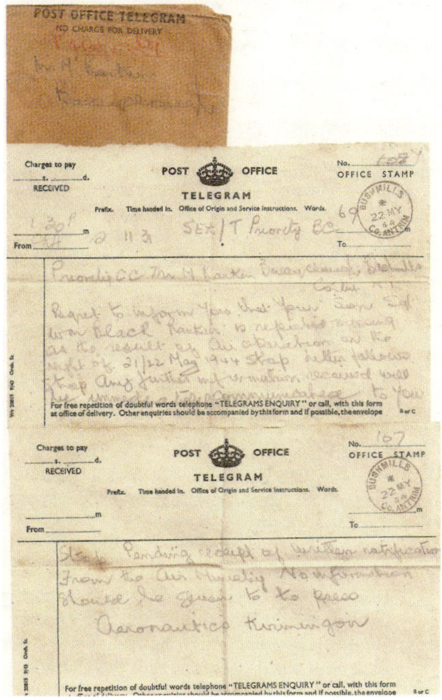

POST OFFICE TELEGRAM
NO CHARGE FOR DELIVERY

Charges to pay ______ s. ______ d.
RECEIVED

POST OFFICE
TELEGRAM

Prefix. Time handed in. Office of Origin and Service Instructions. Words.

No. ______
OFFICE STAMP
BUSHMILLS 22 MY 44 CO. ANTRIM

1.30 P m
From ______ 2 11 31 SEX/T Priority CC 69
To ______

Priority CC Mrs M Rankin ... Bushmills Co Antrim

Regret to inform you that your son Sgt William Black Rankin is reported missing as the result of air operations on the night of 21/22 May 1944 stop letter follows stop any further information received will be ... to you

For free repetition of doubtful words telephone "TELEGRAMS ENQUIRY" or call, with this form at office of delivery. Other enquiries should be accompanied by this form and if possible, the envelope

Charges to pay ______ s. ______ d.
RECEIVED

POST OFFICE
TELEGRAM

Prefix. Time handed in. Office of Origin and Service Instructions. Words.

No. 107
OFFICE STAMP
BUSHMILLS 22 MY 44 CO. ANTRIM

______ m
From ______
To ______

Stop pending receipt of written notification from the Air Ministry no information should be given to the press

Aeronautics Kimmington

For free repetition of doubtful words telephone "TELEGRAMS ENQUIRY" or call, with this form

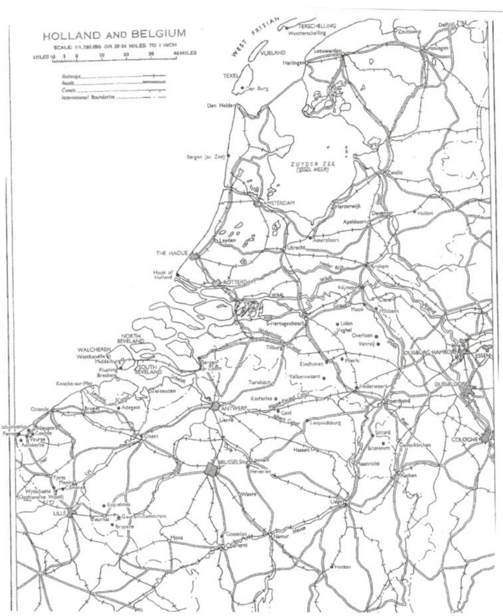

BOMBER COMMAND

No. 166 Squadron

Motto: "Tenacity".
Badge: A bulldog affrontée. The bulldog was chosen because of its reputation for courage and tenacity.
Authority: King George VI, September 1944.

No. 166 Squadron was formed at Bircham Newton, Norfolk, on 13th June 1918, for heavy bombing, and in the following September became the first mobilising unit of No. 27 Group which then began to prepare for long-distance raids into Germany. The squadron personnel were carefully selected, and the pilots and observers, many of them from night-bombing FE2b squadrons in France, underwent a special course at the School of Navigation at Andover. The squadron was to be equipped with the Handley Page V/1500 four-engined bomber - unofficially known as the Super Handley - with which it was hoped, Berlin would be reached from the base in Britain. The first V/1500 flew in May 1918, but was wrecked on test soon afterwards. The Armistice intervened before the squadron could be completely mobilised. Only three V/1500s were ready for use.

The squadron was re-formed in November 1936, as a heavy-bomber squadron equipped with Handley Page Heyford aircraft. It became part of an air observers' school in June 1938, than a Group pool squadron about May 1939 and by the outbreak of the Second World War was flying Whitleys. Soon after the outbreak of war it became a No. 6 Group training squadron. It remained as such until April 1940, and then merged with No. 97 Squadron and SHQ Abingdon to form No. 10 OTU.

No. 166 was re-formed in January 1943, at Kirmington, Lincolnshire - again as a bomber squadron. It remained based at Kirmington throughout the remainder of the war and, flying Wellingtons and Lancasters, participated in many major raids, and also played an active part in Gardening (minelaying). The squadron won at least two DSOs, two CGMs, 117 DFCs and 108 DFMs in the Second World War.

Bomber Command WWII Bases:

- Leconfield : Jan 1937-Sep 1939
- Abingdon : Sep 1939-Apr 1940
- Detachment at Jurby from Feb 1940 onwards.

In 4.40 sqdn merged with No. 97 Sqdn & SHQ Abingdon to form No. 10 OTU. Re-formed 27.1,43 as No. 166(B) Sqdn from home echelons of Nos. 142 & 150(B) Sqdns at

- Kirmington : Jan 1943 onwards

Bomber Command WWII Aircraft:

Telephone No.: GERRARD 9234
Trunk Calls and Telegraphic Address: "AIR MINISTRY," LONDON

AIR MINISTRY,
(Casualty Branch),
73-77 OXFORD STREET,
LONDON, W.1

P.417446/5/P.4.A.2.

30 May, 1944

Sir,

I am commanded by the Air Council to express to you their great regret on learning that your son, Sergeant William Black Rankin, Royal Air Force, is missing as the result of air operations on the night of 21st/22nd May, 1944, when a Lancaster aircraft in which he was flying as mid-upper gunner set out to bomb Duisburg and failed to return.

This does not necessarily mean that he is killed or wounded, and if he is a prisoner of war he should be able to communicate with you in due course. Meanwhile enquiries are being made through the International Red Cross Committee, and as soon as any definite news is received you will be at once informed.

/If any information

M. Rankin, Esq.,
Ballyclough,
Bushmills,
County Antrim,
Northern Ireland.

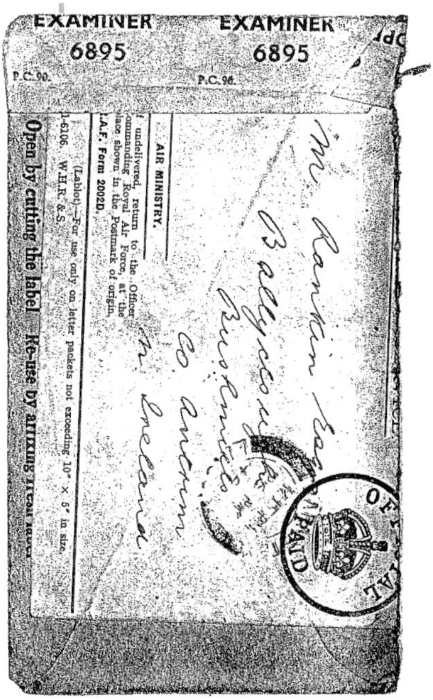

CONFIDENTIAL NOTICE.

The names of all who lose their lives or are wounded or reported missing while serving with the Royal Air Force will appear in the official casualty lists published from time to time in the Press.

Any publication of the date, place or circumstances of a casualty and particularly any reference to the unit concerned, might give valuable information to the enemy, and for this reason, only the name, rank and Service number are included in the official lists.

Relatives are particularly requested, in the national interest, to ensure that any notices published privately do not disclose the date, place or circumstances of the casualty, or the unit.

The Press have been asked to co-operate in ensuring that no information of value to the enemy is published.

Any premature reference in the Press to those reported "missing" may jeopardise their chance of evading capture if they have survived without falling into enemy hands.

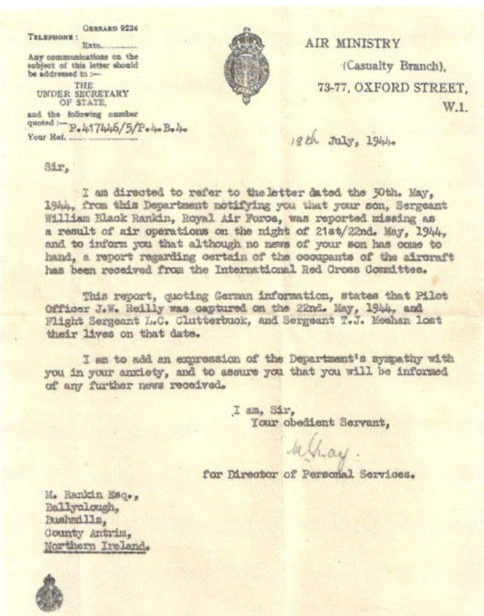

TELEPHONE: GERRARD 9234
Extn.
Any communications on the subject of this letter should be addressed to :—
THE UNDER SECRETARY OF STATE,
and the following number quoted :— P.417446/5/P.4.B.4.
Your Ref.

AIR MINISTRY
(Casualty Branch),
73-77, OXFORD STREET,
W.1.

18th July, 1944.

Sir,

I am directed to refer to the letter dated the 30th. May, 1944, from this Department notifying you that your son, Sergeant William Black Rankin, Royal Air Force, was reported missing as a result of air operations on the night of 21st/22nd. May, 1944, and to inform you that although no news of your son has come to hand, a report regarding certain of the occupants of the aircraft has been received from the International Red Cross Committee.

This report, quoting German information, states that Pilot Officer J.W. Reilly was captured on the 22nd. May, 1944, and Flight Sergeant L.C. Clutterbuck, and Sergeant T.J. Meehan lost their lives on that date.

I am to add an expression of the Department's sympathy with you in your anxiety, and to assure you that you will be informed of any further news received.

I am, Sir,
Your obedient Servant,

for Director of Personal Services.

M. Rankin Esq.,
Ballyclough,
Bushmills,
County Antrim,
Northern Ireland.

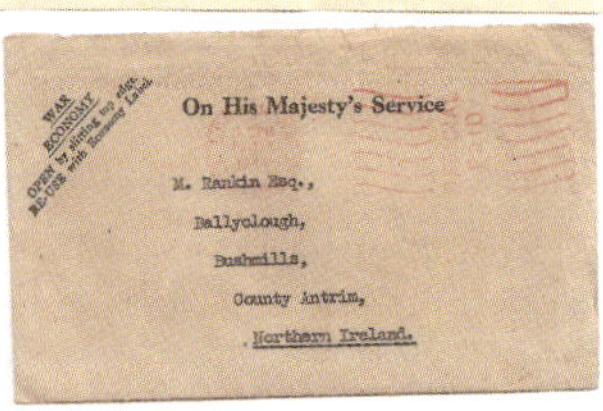

WAR ECONOMY
OPEN by slitting top edge.
RE-USE with Economy Label.

On His Majesty's Service

M. Rankin Esq.,
Ballyclough,
Bushmills,
County Antrim,
Northern Ireland.

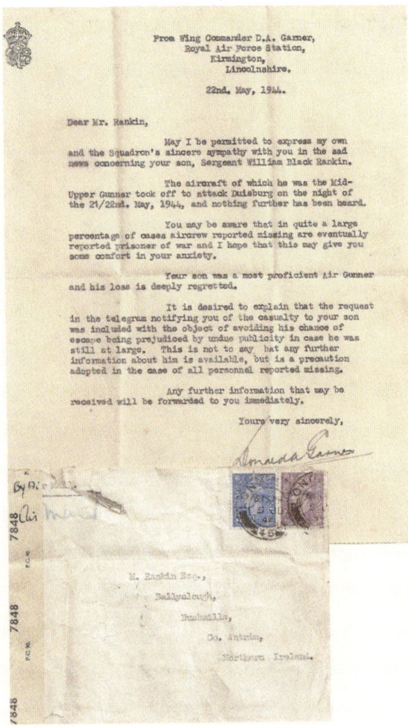

From Wing Commander D.A. Garner,
Royal Air Force Station,
Kirmington,
Lincolnshire.

22nd. May, 1944.

Dear Mr. Rankin,

May I be permitted to express my own and the Squadron's sincere sympathy with you in the sad news concerning your son, Sergeant William Black Rankin.

The aircraft of which he was the Mid-Upper Gunner took off to attack Duisburg on the night of the 21/22nd. May, 1944, and nothing further has been heard.

You may be aware that in quite a large percentage of cases aircrew reported missing are eventually reported prisoner of war and I hope that this may give you some comfort in your anxiety.

Your son was a most proficient Air Gunner and his loss is deeply regretted.

It is desired to explain that the request in the telegram notifying you of the casualty to your son was included with the object of avoiding his chance of escape being prejudiced by undue publicity in case he was still at large. This is not to say that any further information about him is available, but is a precaution adopted in the case of all personnel reported missing.

Any further information that may be received will be forwarded to you immediately.

Yours very sincerely,

7848

M. Rankin Esq.,
Ballyclough,
Bushmills,
Co. Antrim,
Northern Ireland.

Back Row: Rachel Stewart, Jeanie Fleming, Sarah Morton, Lily McAll, Maggie Morton, Molly Dunlop, Sadie McFaul.
Second Row: George Dunlop, Sam Steele, Tommy McKay, Samuel McElnay, David Taggart, Betty Booth, George Walker, Tommy McLean, James Burns,
Third Row: Jamie Johnstone, Joyce Johnstone, Jean McCready, Betty Dunlop, Mary Campbell, Annie King, Millie Holmes, Nellie Morton
Fourth Row: Willie McAuley, ***Willie Rankin****, Mat McLean, Billy Holmes, John Stewart*

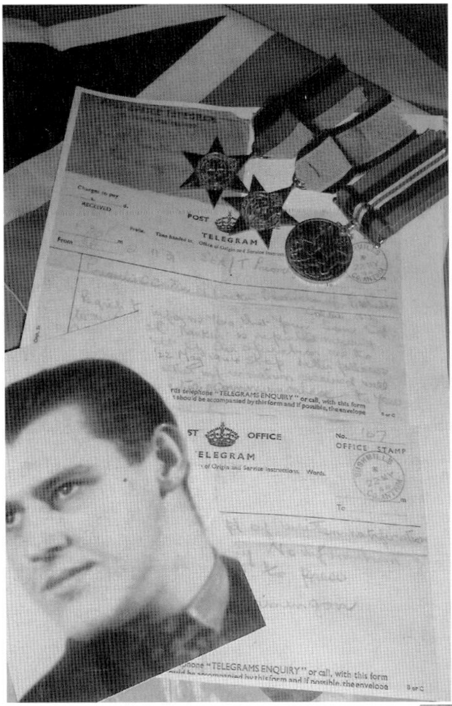

William Rankin Telegram

William Rankin Medals

Harry Elliott

Sergeant 7046131

1st Bn., Royal Irish Fusiliers

Died Friday 20th October, 1944

Harry Elliott was the youngest son of Mr and Mrs John Elliott of Turfahun. His brother James Alexander was also killed in action on 31st March, 1945.

KILLED IN ACTION

Elliott- Killed in action in Italy, October, 1944, Sergeant Harry Elliott, Royal Irish Fusiliers, Youngest son of Mr and Mrs John Elliott of Turfahun Bushmills.

What would I give to clasp his hand,
His dear kind face to see.
To hear his voice, to see his smile
that meant so much to me.

Deeply regretted and sadly missed by his sorrowing wife and little son. Ballytober, Priestland, Co. Antrim.

Harry was a farm labourer before joining the army in 1940. His brother James and his twin brother George served in the R.A.F. and his sister Ester served in the W.A.A.F.

THE ITALIAN CAMPAIGN

On 13th of October 1944, the 1st Bn., were in castle De Rio, then by the 18th they had advanced to Apollenora, the battalion was involved in a battle attacking two villages called Spinella and Spandura.

At first a day attack is planned but this was cancelled and replaced by a night attack. At the end of the day the casualties recorded were 22 killed 61 wounded and 85 missing.

Harry Elliott is buried in Santerno Cemetery, Italy. There are 287 burials in this cemetery

Santerno War Cemetery, Italy

John Elliott married Henrietta Johnston

- John
- Lizzie
- William
- Henrietta
- **JAMES ALEXANDER KIA Norway 31 March 1945**
- Elias
- Thomas
- George
- **Harry KIA Italy 20th October 1944**
- Hester

CASTLECATT PRIMARY SCHOOL

FIRST ROW; Edwin Getty, Alan Graham, James Glass, Stewart McKendry Mac Acheson, Dan Kane.

SECOND ROW; Margaret Barr. Jeannie Moore, Jim Getty, Dorothy Getty, Mamie McKendry, Lizzie Walker, Alice Wilkinson, Minnie McKeown, Margaret McCurdy, Dorothy McCurdy, Myrtle Wysner, Sarah McAuley, Betty Twadle, Mary Law, Violet Houston George Graham

THIRD ROW; Henry Moore, Sinclair Callaghan, Jeannie Barr, Annie Twaddle, Annie Patterson, Annie Hill, Frances Patterson, Teenie Neil, Tillie McLean, Mary Moore, Maggie McAuley, Jeannie Neill, Annie McKeown, Evelyn Getty, GEORGE ELLIOTT, HARRY ELLIOTT.

FOURTH ROW; Willie Callaghan, Tommy McKeown, Molly Twaddle, Jeannie McLean, Annie Moore, Rena Getty, Bell Graham, Nellie McAuley, Molly Hanna, Hester Elliott, Tilda Barr, Maggie Walker, Sylvia Kane, Annie Callaghan, Tillie Mary Kane.

FIFTH ROW; Willie McKeown, Tommy Laverty, Noel Christie, Norman McKeown, Jim Walker, Tommy Elliott, Jim Laverty, Willie Hanna, Jim Kane, Stanley Callaghan, Hugh Barr, Sam Kane.

BACK ROW; Jim Christie, Eddie Wilmont Johnny Stewart

William Clyde

Sergeant 1798065

106 Sqd. Royal Air Force

Died Monday, 6th November, 1944

Age 20

William Patrick Clyde was the son of William and Frances Clyde of Stanalane, Bushmills. His elder brother James also served in the R.A.F. William had been in the building trade before enlisting.

BUSHMILLS AIRMAN KILLED IN ACTION

Mrs William Clyde, Stanalane, Bushmills, has been informed by the Air Ministry that her son, Sergeant Air-Gunner William Clyde, who had been reported missing in November, 1944, is now reported killed while taking part in his ninth operational flight over enemy territory. About two years ago Sergeant Clyde volunteered for service in the R.A.F. as an air-gunner, and after completing his training he was stationed in England.

His elder brother Corporal James Clyde, who is at present home on leave, is also serving in the R.A.F. which he joined before the outbreak of war. Their father has been employed on war work in England for a number of years.

COLERAINE CHRONICLE

William is commemorated on his parents grave in Bushmills R.C. Church.

WILLIAM CLYDE

Sergeant William Clyde was serving with 106 squadron based in Lincolnshire. He was the mid upper gunner on a Lancaster bomber, Mark 1 serial number LL953 ZN-O which took off from the airfield at Metheringham at 16.30 hours on 6th November, 1944 to take part on an attack on the Dortmund-Ems and Mitteland canal systems near Gravenhorst. Nothing was heard from the aircraft after take off. The aircraft crashed near Ahuas with the loss of all her crew.

William had been hospitalised earlier in September due to wounds from flak to his shoulder while on an operational flight over enemy territory.

On that night of the 6th November 1944, 228 Lancasters and 7 Mosquitoes were dispatched on the canal attack. Difficulty was experienced in marking the target, and the controller gave orders for the attack to be abandoned.

There was no low cloud, but weather conditions were hazy and very dark, some of the aircraft dropped 14 x 1000 lb. bombs over the target.

Flak defences were encountered over the target and on the homeward route. 10 Lancasters were missing.

The crew of the Lancaster number LL953ZN-O were originally buried at Nienborg but later re consecrated in the Reichswald Forest Cemetery.

THE CREW

182745 Flying Officer Conrad Denis Neale - Pilot

1520932 Sergeant Sydney Napier Hilder - Bomb Aimer

1323620 Flight Sergeant Walter Hardy - Navigator

1674487 Sergeant Robert Lionel Armstrong - Flight Engineer

1785330 Sergeant William Meikle Mc Intyre- Wireless Operator/Air Gunner

1825824 Sergeant James MacGregor Coll - Rear Gunner

and

1798865 Sergeant William Patrick Clyde-Mid Upper Gunner.

There are 7580 burials in this cemetery.

Matt Clyde, wearing his brother William's medals

BOMBER COMMAND

No. 106 Squadron

Motto: "Pro libertate" ("For freedom").
Badge: A lion sejant, rampant, holding a banner charged with an astral crown. A lion sejant, rampant, holding a banner is based on the crest of the County Borough of Doncaster, the squadron being stationed near there at the time of adopting the badge.
Authority: King George VI, February 1941.

No 106 Squadron, RFC, was formed at Andover, Hampshire, on 30th September 1917, and from May 1918, onwards served in Ireland as an army co-operation squadron. It was disbanded in 1919 and next appeared in June 1938, when it was re-formed as No 106 (Bomber) Squadron.

At the outbreak of the Second World War the squadron was flying Hampdens with No. 5 Group, and until early 1941 had a training role. It then reverted to front-line status and began regular night bombing operations against Fortress Europe.

After a short spell with Manchesters, No 106 converted to Lancasters in the early summer of 1942 (but it did not become converted completely to Lancasters before some of the Manchesters had participated in the 1,000-bomber raids on Cologne, Essen and Bremen). In October it contributed 10 Lancasters to No. 5 Group's epic dusk raid on Le Creusot and two more (one of them piloted by Wing Commander Guy Gibson who was then No 106's CO) to the subsidiary raid on Montchanin. In 1943 it took part in the first "shuttle-bombing" raids (when the targets were Friedrichshafen and Spezia) and the famous attack on Peenemunde. Among the targets attacked in 1944 were a coastal gun battery at St. Pierre du Mont and the V1 storage sites in the caves at St. Leu d'Esserent. In December 1944, it made a 1,900-mile round trip to bomb the German Baltic Fleet at Gdynia, while in March 1945, it was represented in the bomber force that so pulverised the defences of Wesel just before the Rhine crossing that Commandos were able to seize the town with only 36 casualties. In April 1945, came the last of the squadron's operations against the enemy - a bombing attack on an oil refinery at Vallo (Tonsberg) in Norway, and a simultaneous minelaying expedition to the Oslo fjord.

During the Second World War No 106 Squadron operated on 496 nights and 46 days, flying 5,834 operational sorties. In so doing it lost 187 aircraft - a percentage loss on sorties flown of 3.21 - but on the credit side its gunners claimed 20 enemy aircraft destroyed, 3 probably destroyed and 29 damaged. A total of 267 decorations were won by the squadron, including a Victoria Cross awarded to Sergeant NC Jackson for conspicuous bravery during an attack on Schweinfurt on 26/27th April 1944.

Bomber Command WWII Bases:

- Thornaby : Oct 1938-Sep 1939
- Detached to Evanton in Aug 1939 & from there moved, early in Sep 1939, to:
- Cottesmore : Sep 1939-Oct 1939
- Finningley : Oct 1939-Feb 1941
- Coningsby : Feb 1941-Sep 1942
- Syerston : Sep 1942-Nov 1943
- Metheringham : Nov 1943 onwards

VICTORY

I am sending you someone precious
Please treat him kindly and fair,
He's a package for "Somewhere in Britain"
To the R.A.F. with care.

I've wrapped him with prayers and good wishes
In a cellophane all of my own
And I trust with Gods help it will keep him
Until he gets safe back home.

To you he's just one of a thousand
And they say that life is cheap
But to me he's my only laddie
And a package I'd like to keep.

I lend him to you to hasten
The dawn of a better day
When justice and right will have triumphed
And tyranny passed quite away.

And when all the battles are over
And victory has set Nations free
No matter how worn or damaged
Please send back my
Package to me.

A. MOTHER

Albert Morton

Fusilier 6470178

1st Bn., Royal Fusiliers (City Of London Regiment)

Died Wednesday 6th December, 1944

Fusilier Albert Morton was only twenty eight years old when he was killed in action in Italy.

He had joined the Royal Fusiliers and was connected with The London Irish.

The 1st battalion of the Royal Fusiliers had been in India at the outbreak of world war two. It served in the Sudan, Syria, Basra and Palestine and in September, 1943 went to Italy as part of the 176 Infantry Brigade.

It took part in much of the fighting and from July, 1944 was part of the force following the German army on its orderly retreat up the Italian Peninsula.

By September 1944 the battalion was in the area of Mount Bitella, on the 6th December the Germans were thought to be evacuating to villages S. Mchele and S.Stefano. A fighting patrol was sent out re reconnoitre forward. The Battalion war diary records fighting taking place and that two men were injured. It was at this time that Albert died.

Albert was the youngest son of Robert and Elizabeth Morton, and was brought up in Ballytober. Albert had joined up in 1940 and before that was employed in the Royal Hotel,Giants Causeway. He had served for 4 years in North Africa and the central Mediterranean.

Six brothers have served in the Great War and the Second World War.

He was the third brother to pay the supreme sacrifice, the other two were John, killed in 1915 in the Dardenelles Campaign and stoker Samuel Morton, royal navy who lost his life at sea in 1942. His nephew, Robert also lost his life on active duty.

Albert was married and left behind a little son, Ted, aged three years.

FUSILIER ALBERT MORTON

Albert had left Ballytober and gone to work in England. He lived in Kentish Town, London. He joined up in 1940 and was stationed near Ashford in Kent, then Exmouth in Devon. Albert

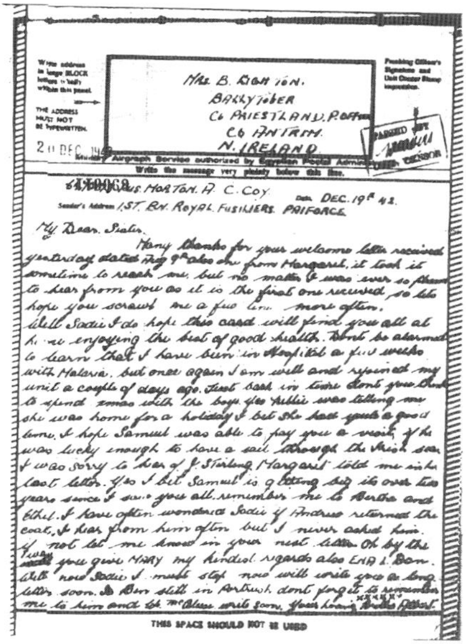

Write address in large BLOCK letters boldly within this panel. THE ADDRESS MUST NOT BE TYPEWRITTEN.

MRS. B. RIGHTON.
BALLYTOBER
Co PRIESTLAND. P. Office
Co ANTRIM.
N. IRELAND

Passing Officer's Signature and Unit Censor Stamp impression.

20 DEC 1942

PASSED BY CENSOR

Military Airgraph Service authorised by Egyptian Postal Administration. Write the message very plainly below this line.

6470068 FUS. MORTON. A. C. COY. Date DEC. 19th 42.
Sender's Address 1ST. BN. ROYAL FUSILIERS. PAIFORCE.

My Dear Sister,

Many thanks for your welcome letter received yesterday dated Aug 9th also one from Margaret, it took it sometime to reach me, but no matter I was ever so pleased to hear from you as it is the first one received, so lets hope you scrawl me a few lines more often.

Well Sadie I do hope this card will find you all at home enjoying the best of good health. Dont be alarmed to learn that I have been in Hospital a few weeks with Malaria, but once again I am well and rejoined my unit a couple of days ago. Just back in time dont you think to spend xmas with the boys. Yes Tillie was telling me she was home for a holiday I bet she had quite a good time. I hope Samuel was able to pay you a visit, if he was lucky enough to have a sail through the Irish sea. I was sorry to hear of J. Stirling Margaret told me in her last letter. Yes I bet Samuel is getting big its over two years since I seen you all. remember me to Bertha and Ethel. I have often wondered Sadie if Andrew returned the coat, I hear from him often but I never asked him. If not let me know in your next letter. Oh by the way give MARY my kindest regards also EMA & Ben. Well now Sadie I must stop now will write you a long letter soon. Is Ben still in Portrush dont forget to remember me to him and Mr. McAleese write soon. Your loving Brother Albert. xxxxx

THIS SPACE SHOULD NOT BE USED

kept in touch with his family, and you can tell when reading his letters that he really missed home.

After being home on leave in 1940 he spent a weekend with his brother Samuel. He tells of all the drill and exercises that they do in camp, guarding bridges and the Royal Military Canal.

They have two suits, one canvass for doing drill and the other for dress, which Albert describes as very tidy but very warm. They are also issued with two pairs of boots, one pair of gaiters, three pairs of socks, steel hat, rifle and bayonet, hair brush, shaving brush, clothes brush, overcoat, button brush, drinking flask and one pair of slippers for doing P.T. also three blankets.

On the day of writing this letter they had all been inoculated, twice on one arm and once on the other.

Once on leave in London he met up with brother Samuel again, along with Nellie, Alice, Effie and Margaret. They had a great time together and he found it very hard to leave them.

While leaving Andrew to Euston Station he saw Willie McAllister who had just joined the Navy, and who was married to Sissie Mullholland.

In one of his many letters home, both himself and Samuel were anxious to hear from home, as the mail had not been delivered and they were worried. Not long after, Albert's battalion were not allowed to leave the barracks, they were all posted to trenches and had to hold this position at all costs. They didn't think that jerry would come over, but three of the boys were killed by a bomb. There was no end to the planes.

In one of the many letters home to his sister Margaret (Mrs W. Scott)., he tells of the boiling hot sun and sands of North Africa and the heat in Italy. How friendly the Italians were, welcoming them with a glass of wine as they went along and not forgetting the beautiful girls! He misses home and can't wait for the war to end.

Albert was devastated when he heard the news that his brother Samuel had been killed in action. He wrote home to his family asking them to be brave and not to worry about him . . .

MRS. W. SCOTT.
17. CHURCH STREET.
592601 BUSHMILLS. Co. ANTRIM
N. IRELAND.

Christmas Greetings from The Eighth Army

"Together, you and I we will see this thing through to the end" ALBERT. WITH LOVE TO ALL.

Albert Morton is buried in Faenza war cemetery, Italy and commemorated Dunluce Parish Church memorial.

Faenza Cemetery was formed in the winter of 1944 for the burial of those who were killed in the fighting before the allied advance was renewed in April 1945. There are 1152 burials in this Commonwealth Cemetery from the Second World War.

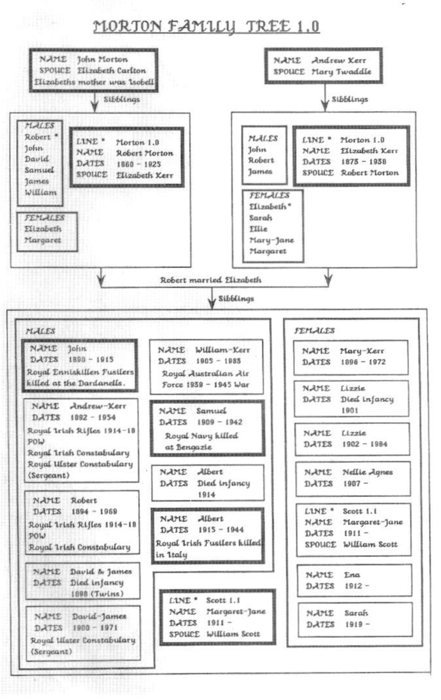

Back Row: Rachel Stewart, Jeanie Fleming, Sarah Morton, Lily McAll, Maggie Morton, Molly Dunlop, Sadie McFaul.
Second Row: George Dunlop, Sam Steele, Tommy McKay, Samuel McElnay, David Taggart, Betty Booth, George Walker, Tommy McLean, James Burns,
Third Row: Jamie Johnstone, Joyce Johnstone, Jean McCready, Betty Dunlop, Mary Campbell, Annie King, Millie Holmes, Nellie Morton
Fourth Row: Willie McAuley, ***Willie Rankin****, Mat McLean, Billy Holmes, John Stewart*

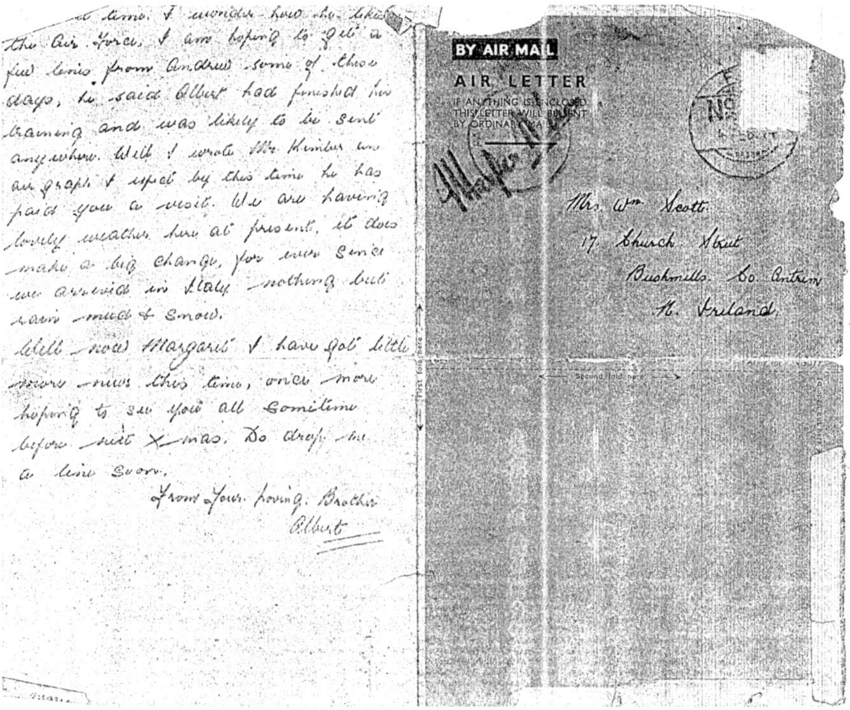

...d time. I wonder how he likes
the Air Force. I am hoping to get a
few lines from Andrew some of these
days, he said Albert had finished his
training and was likely to be sent
anywhere. Well I wrote Mr. Kimber an
air graph & expect by this time he has
paid you a visit. We are having
lovely weather here at present, it does
make a big change, for ever since
we arrived in Italy nothing but
rain mud & snow.
Well now Margaret I have got little
more news this time, once more
hoping to see you all sometime
before next X-mas. Do drop me
a line soon.
From Your loving Brother
Albert

BY AIR MAIL
AIR LETTER
IF ANYTHING IS ENCLOSED THIS LETTER WILL BE SENT BY ORDINARY MAIL

Mrs. Wm Scott
17 Church Street
Bushmills Co. Antrim
N. Ireland

First fold here
Second fold here

James Alexander Elliott

Sergeant 1900093 Air Gunner

299 Sqd., Royal Air Force Volunteer Reserve

Died Saturday 31st March, 1945

James Alexander Elliott came from Turfahun, Bushmills. He was the fifth child in a family of ten children. His brother Harry was also killed in action, and is buried in Santerno Cemetery, Italy.

James went to school in Castlecatt and worked to a local farmer Charles Mcvicker from Craigahulliar. He attended Bushmills Presbyterian Church, where there is a brass memorial bearing his name.

On the night of 30th-31st March 1945 close to Vierli in Vegaarshei in Southern Norway, Germans shot down a short sterling MK IV. The code name for this operation was "Snaffle 6 or Spinach"

The plane flew out of the airfield Shepherds Grove in England on 30th March at 9'o clock and the drop zone was NB 502. It was bringing supplies for the Norwegian resistance, Milorg.

On that plane were Pilot Trevor Roper D.F.C. Navigator H.W. Ricketts Telegraphist P.S. Brinkworth, Flymaster K.C. Hayward and Air Gunner Sgt. J.A. Elliott. A/c missing is noted on the official report. The Norwegian resistance Milorg in telemark group, named "starlight" district 16 was waiting for the plane in drop zone NB 502.

It never arrived. The airmen were shot down, the plane crashed in flames into the forest where it made a deep hole in the ground.

The Germans recovered the bodies and they were taken to the local church in Sondeled where they were buried together.

A local man aged 18 at the time witnessed the crash from his bedroom window. He told us of seeing the plane come down and the awful noise that it made when it hit the ground. Both him and his parents tried to get to the site but they were held back by the intense heat and the German soldiers. It is a memory that never leaves his mind, he visits the crash site often, and lays flowers there.

James is commemorated on Bushmills Presbyterian Church Memorial

John Elliott married Henrietta Johnston

- John
- Lizzie
- William
- Henrietta
- **JAMES ALEXANDER KIA Norway 31 March 1945**
- Elias
- Thomas
- George
- **Harry KIA Italy 20th October 1944**
- Hester

Ved minnesmerket etter avdukingen den 8. mai 1983.
Milorg. gruppe D 16 fra Telemark som ventet forgjeves på transportflyet natten til 31 mars 1945. Fra venstre: Kompani Linge-løytnant Arne Kjelstrup, Eldar Hagen, Knut Øverli, Arne Johnsen, Sigurd Dalane, Edvin Antonsen, Bjarne Venaas, Erling Mathisen, Oskar Hagen, Olaf Hvasshovd og Arne Lundby.

Foto: Lodin Aasbø

Wing Commander K.O. Harding taler ved bautaen 8. mai 1983.

Foto: Lodin Aasbo

"They come in the night"

BUCKINGHAM PALACE

The Queen and I offer you our heartfelt sympathy in your great sorrow.

We pray that your country's gratitude for a life so nobly given in its service may bring you some measure of consolation.

George R.I

J. Elliott, Esq.

The Under-Secretary of State for Air presents his compliments and by Command of the Air Council has the honour to transmit the enclosed Awards granted for service in the war of 1939-45.

The Council share your sorrow that

SERGEANT J.A. ELLIOTT

in respect of whose service these Awards are granted did not live to receive them.

James Alexander's nephew John Elliott

*Parts of plane **still** at wreckage site*

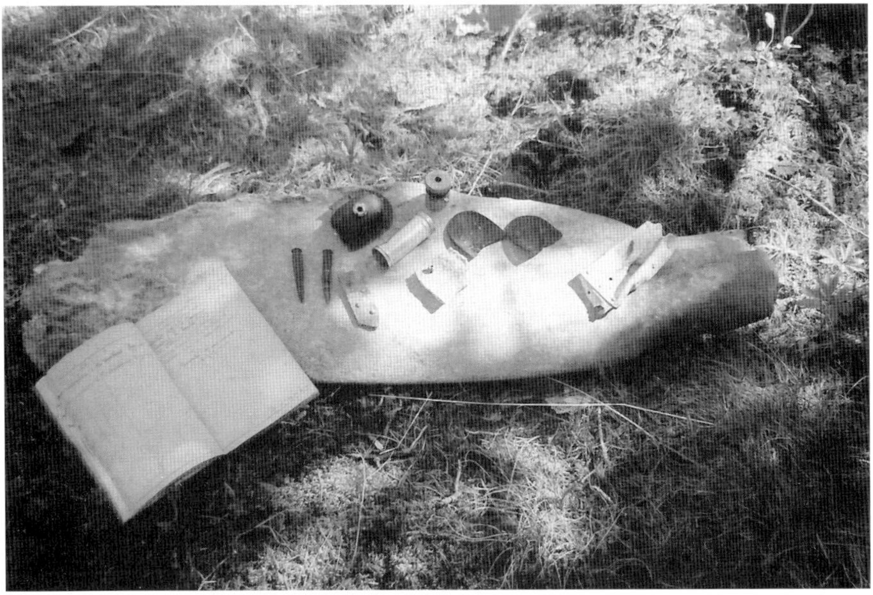

Rudder of plane, with log book and crews personal belongings

James Alexander Elliott

Brinkwork, Elliott, Roper, Peat, Ricketts

John McMullan Quigg

Able Seaman
D/JX 302542

Royal Navy

Died 24th May, 1945

Johns parents were Robert and Elizabeth Quigg of Araboy, Bushmills. He was 24 years of age when he died in the Ulster Volunteer Hospital in Belfast.

He had served with the Royal Navy in Sicily and was wounded in the body and leg. He was taken to an American Field Hospital where his leg was amputated. On returning to England he was hospitalised. His mother was granted a permit to see him, but she was too infirm to travel.

John did not survive his injuries and was returned home to the Ulster Volunteer Hospital where he later died of his injuries. He is buried in Toberkeigh Presbyterian Churchyard.

Violet Florence Moore

Leading Aircraft Woman
2099386

Women's Aux. Air Force

Died Tuesday 19th February, 1946

Violet Florence was the third daughter of Thomas James Moore and Euphemia Jane Moore of Portbalintrae.

Violets sisters were Mary Elizabeth and Sarah Jane, brothers were James, Robert who served in the Royal Navy as a Radio Operator, William who also served in the Royal Navy as a Signalman and John who lives at Dundarave.

Violet was educated at Lacklum School in Donegal, this is where she had been born.

The family once lived in Drumholm Donegal where their father Thomas was a Landsteward to an English Judge. They left Drumholm in 1941 and moved to Greengables, Portballintrae.

Violet was only 24 years of age when she died of an illness while on active service. She is buried in Drumholm old Church of Ireland graveyard in Donegal.

Robert Morton

Fusilier 1444604

Royal Inniskilling Fusiliers

Died Monday 1st July, 1946

Age 20

Robert was the eldest son of Robert and Minnie Morton of Ballytober, Priestland. He died on active service while stationed in England, due to a drowning accident.

He joined the Royal Ulster Rifles Airborne Division in 1943, and later transferred to the Royal Inniskilling Fusiliers.

While serving with the Fusiliers in Germany he received wounds.

Fusilier Morton was to be demobbed the next month and was looking forward, as were his family to his homecoming.

His father worked in England on war work and his younger brother William was stationed there, with the army. Three of his fathers brothers made the supreme sacrifice, John the eldest son in the Great War, Samuel and Albert in the Second World War.

Robert is not commemorated on our war memorial in Bushmills at present, but after the memorial has been refurbished in the near future, this I hope will be rectified.

THE FUNERAL

There was a large attendance at the funeral of fusilier Robert Morton which took place on Sunday afternoon from the residence of his parents, Ballytober, Priestland, to Dunluce Presbyterian churchyard.

His death took place in England at the beginning of the previous week as the result of a drowning accident.

He belongs to a family which has a proud record of service in the forces in the 1914-1918 and 1939-1945 wars.

The services in the home and at the graveside were conducted by rev. S Alexander B.A.

Many beautiful wreaths were laid on the grave, and included, in addition to those from his family and relatives, a large number from chums and friends from the district where he was well known.

The sympathy of the entire neighbourhood is extended to his mother, father, brother and sisters in their tragic bereavement.

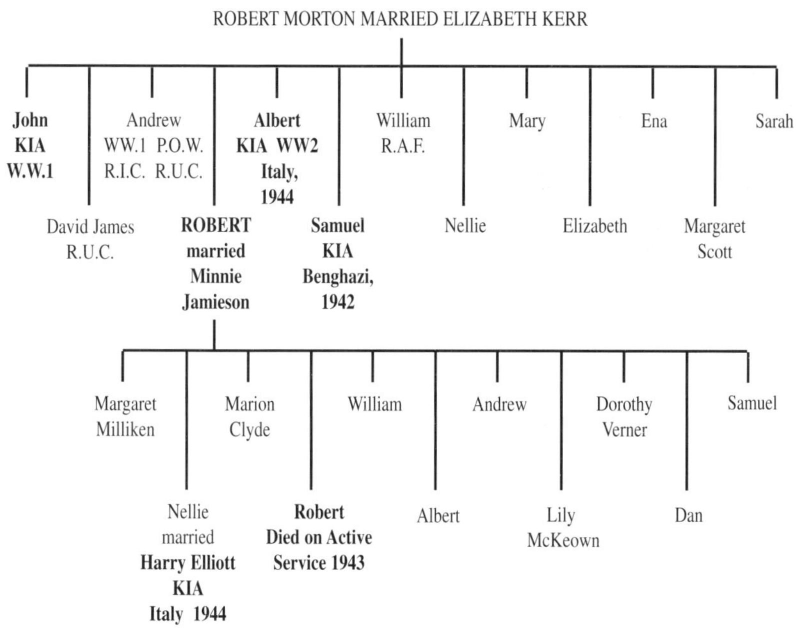

WAR AND PEACE

The poppies slowly flutter down,
In silence here we stand,
Each petal in remembrance
To the fallen of our land.

The poppy knows no barriers
No divisions ever sought,
Together as one nation
For one cause they fought.

It represents each nation
Poppy red their blood was shed,
It brings us all together
In remembrance of our dead.

The poppy is the symbol
A remembrance of war and peace,
The terrible conflict that war brings
And the hope that all wars may cease.

Frank scott
16 Hamill Terrace
Bushmills.

David Smiley

Private 14476508

2nd. Bn., Queens Own Cameron Highlanders

Died Sunday 11th May, 1947

David Montgomery Smiley was only 19 years old when he died. He was the son of Mrs T. Donnelly of Store Row, Bushmills.

David had joined Her Majesty's Forces when he was 18 and after training and other duties, he had been sent on overseas service.

He was stationed in Trieste, Italy and that is where he died. His family had received news that he was critically ill as the result of gunshot wounds to the abdomen. A message received a few days later stated that he had died.

David's family at home were deeply saddened by his death, his grandfather Mr. James Smiley of Store Row was an ex service man himself. Two other young members of the family were in the services, Ernest Smiley at the time was stationed in India and private Cecil Smiley was at home on leave.

David is buried in Udine War Cemetery, Trieste, Italy. Udine was entered by the troops on the 1st May 1945. Soldiers buried in this cemetery include casualties from the last few days of the war some prisoner-of-war air force casualties and burials from 70 British General Hospital which was at Udine from May 1945.

Udine Cemetery has 414 burials.

David is commemorated on Dunluce Parish Memorial.

Samuel Maxwell

Private

Pioneer Corps

Died of the effects of the war,
30th May, 1950

Served in two wars

It was with feelings of deep sorrow that the people of Bushmills district learned of the death of Mr. Samuel Maxwell, at his residence, the cottages, Bushfoot Portballintrae, after a lingering illness through which he maintained his usual cheerful disposition.

He served in two world wars, serving with the Royal Irish Rifles from 1914 to 1918 where he received severe leg wounds. He again volunteered in the 1939-45 war, serving with the A.M.P.C.

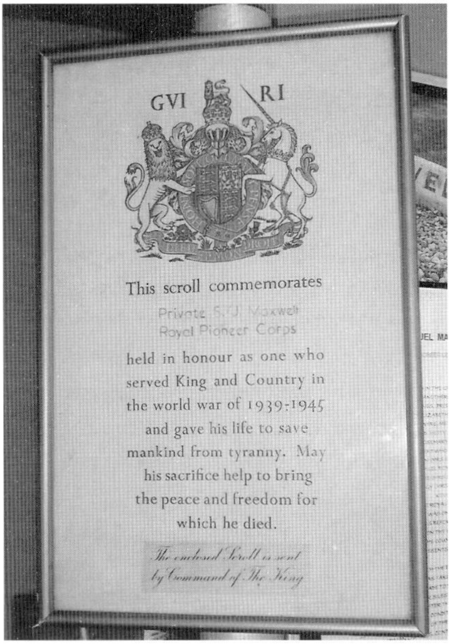

Samuel died of the effects of the harsh treatment he received from his German captives, contrary to the Geneva Convention.

He was taken Prisoner of War at Boulogne, France in May 1940 and remained in captivity until released by the allied forces in 1945.

He was taken to Germany and was made to do hard labour in a salt mine in Upper Silesia for five years.

Many of his comrades in the prison camp later testified that it was Sam Maxwell who, by his cheery nature

PRISONER OF WAR.

Mrs. Maxwell has been notified through the Red Cross that her husband, Charles Maxwell, who was previously reported missing, is now a prisoner of war in Hong Kong. Charles is a son of Mr. Robert Maxwell, Portballintrae. His brother, Samuel, is a prisoner in Germany, and Robert, another brother, made the supreme sacrifice in France. Mr. Robert Maxwell, father of these three gallant young men, was, since the opening of the Bushmills and Giant's Causeway Tramway, employed by the company until about three years ago, and was one of the first to drive the old steam engines of those days prior to the inauguration of the electric system. Latterly he was in charge of the generating station at the Walkmill Falls on the River Bush.

and his expressed confidence in an allied victory even in the darkest hours kept up their morale and gave them renewed hope.

From leaving school except during the years of his war service up to 1939 Mr Maxwell was employed by the Giants Causeway-Portrush Electric Tramway Company, being in charge of the Generating Station at the Walkmill.

On his return home in 1945, following a period of rest, he got employment at Coleraine Railway Station and remained there until illness compelled him to give up work.

He was a valued member of Portballintrae l.O.L No. 1142.

In all phases of his life, Sam was most popular and made legions of friends. He was one of a family who gave gallant service to their King and Country.

His eldest brother received severe wounds in the first world war from which he later died.

His brother Robert was killed in action in France around the time that Samuel was taken prisoner in 1940. Still another brother Charlie, who served in the Royal Navy 1939-1945 was for a number of years a prisoner of war in the hands of the Japanese.

On reaching the required age, Sam's eldest son Samuel, joined the Royal Navy and served throughout the war.

The funeral took place to Dunluce Parish Churchyard, the coffin being draped with the Union Jack. A very large and representative attendance included many ex-servicemen and members of the British legion, as well as employees of the Coleraine branch of The Ulster Transport authority.

Amongst the many beautiful floral tributes from relatives and friends, were wreaths from the staff of Coleraine Railway Station, the British Legion and Portballintrae l.O.L No. 1142.

The services in the home, in the church and at the graveside were conducted by Rev F.G. Guy M.A. H.C.F. with his widow two sons and three daughters, sisters, brothers and other relatives there is widespread sympathy.

MAXWELL—In loving memory of our dear father, Robert Maxwell, of Portballintrae, Bushmills, who passed away 20th January, 1943.

Not just to-day, but every day,
In silence we remember.

Ever remembered by his seven daughters and son, Sam (a prisoner of war in Germany).

Samuel is commemorated on Dunluce Parish Church Memorial and Portballintrae Royal Blues L.O.L. No. 1142

Bob Maxwell Married Margaret Thompson

- Meta
- Maud
- Lizzie
- Alex
- Hetty
- May
- Sadie
- **William Jubilee Died of Effects of The Great War 1919**
- **Robert Killed In Action Dunkirk 1940**
  - Lily (Mrs K. Montgomery)
  - Billy
  - Jim
- **Samuel Died of Effects of War 1950**
  - Sam Royal Navy
  - Joan (Mrs A. Graham)
  - Robbie
  - Sadie (Mrs C. Sinclair)
  - Peggy (Mrs R. Taylor)
  - Kevin

Chronicle Feb. 13, 1982

OBITUARY

Mr. Charles Maxwell

Portballintrae

The death of Mr. Charles Maxwell, which took place at his home, 23 Darkfort Drive, Portballintrae, last week, caused widespread sorrow and regret. He was aged 69.

Mr. Maxwell began work at an early age on the Giant's Causeway Tramway, in which his father, Mr. Robert Maxwell, was the engineer in charge of the hydro electric power station at the Walk Mills.

At the age of 17 he joined the Royal Navy, and during the Second World War was captured by the Japanese. For four years he suffered extreme hardship and torture.

After his release, and because of his disability, Mr. Maxwell found it difficult to adjust to normal life.

He became well-known for constructing and flying model aeroplanes and for building model boats.

Mr. Maxwell later did some fishing locally and became a popular figure with visitors and residents alike as quite a character.

Because of heart trouble, he had to accept a less active lifestyle, but he never complained and always managed to keep cheerful.

The funeral, to Dunluce Parish Church on Wednesday of last week, was largely attended, further

testifying to the esteem in which Mr. Maxwell was held.

Chancellor F. G. Guy, rector of Dunluce Parish, assisted by Mr. Colin Sinclair, Diocesan Lay Reader, officiated in the home, in Dunluce church and at the graveside.

Mr. Maxwell, who was predeceased by his wife, Martha, is survived by his two sons, Leonard and Charles, and a brother, Johnnie.

Sisters are Mrs. H. M'Elreavey, Portballintrae; Mrs. A. Pedlow, Belfast; Mrs. S. M'Garry, Canada; and Mrs. E. Gosling, Carlisle.

There are five grandchildren.

William Watt

Pioneer Corps

Died 6th March, 1951

At the outbreak of the second world war, William joined the services for a second time, having served in the Great War. He served with the Pioneer Corps and was honoured with The Kings Badge for loyal service in the forces, together with the ribbon of the 1939-1945 star.

He was a member of Bushmills L.O.L. No. 914 and at the monthly meeting in March 1951, Br. William McNeill the W.M. passed a vote of sympathy to his wife and family.

William was the youngest son of James and Agnes Watt of Portrush. His wife was Sarah and they resided in Store Row Bushmills.

William had two sisters, Sarah Simpson and Florence Galbreath. Florence lived on the Ormeau Road Belfast.

William died in Bannview Hospital, suffering with the effects of the war. He is buried in Dunluce Parish Graveyard. Rev. F.G. Guy assisted at the funeral.

The Pioneer Corps was a British Army combatant Corps used for light engineering tasks. It was raised on 17 th October, 1939 and was renamed the Royal Pioneer Corps by King George V1 for its meritorious work during 1939-1945.

There is reference to the Pioneers in the Book of Nehemiah which states;

> "They which build a wall, and they that bear burdens, with those that laboured, everyone with one of his hands wrought the work, and with the other hand, held a weapon".

Pioneers performed a wide variety of tasks, in all theatres of war. These tasks ranged from handling all types of stores, laying pre-fabricated track on beaches to stretcher bearing.

Samuel Alexander

Royal Artillery

Died 11th September, 1951

Ex-Serviceman's Death

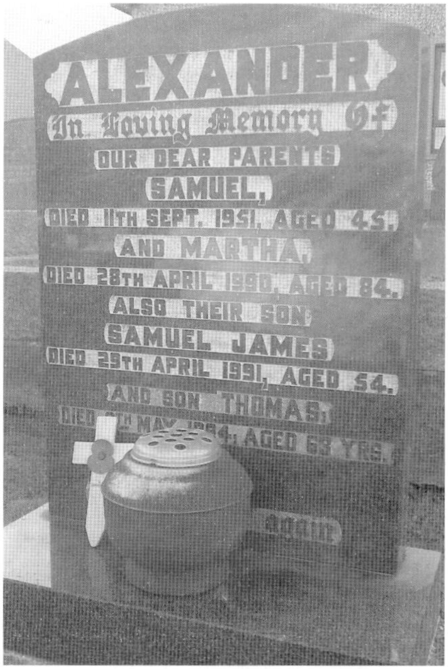

Deep regret was felt at the death of Mr Samuel Alexander at his residence, Upper Main Street Bushmills., following a heart attack. Samuel had been ill for some months.

Shortly after demobilization from the Forces, he found employment in the White House, Portrush. Here he was very popular with his workmates and his employer.

At the outbreak of war in 1939 he joined the Ballymena anti-aircraft regiment, R.A. and served with his

Samuel refereeing a boxing match in Alexandria

Samuel Alexander far right

unit in the Middle East.

While still serving in the Middle East in 1942, he was invalided out of the army. The ship in which he was travelling home, was torpedoed and he lost all his belongings.

He was awarded the 8th Army Star and the Middle East Star.

William left a wife who was the daughter of the late Mr. and Mrs. Thomas McCollum, and a family of seven.

With them and his father and mother Mr. And Mrs. James Alexander Upper Main Street and his brothers and sisters, there is widespread sympathy.

William was buried in his family grave in Bushmills Presbyterian Church Graveyard.

There was a large attendance at the funeral, including many ex-servicemen from the town. A Union Jack draped the coffin on which were beautiful floral tributes from his relatives. Rev. Samuel Eaton M.A. H.C.F. conducted the service.

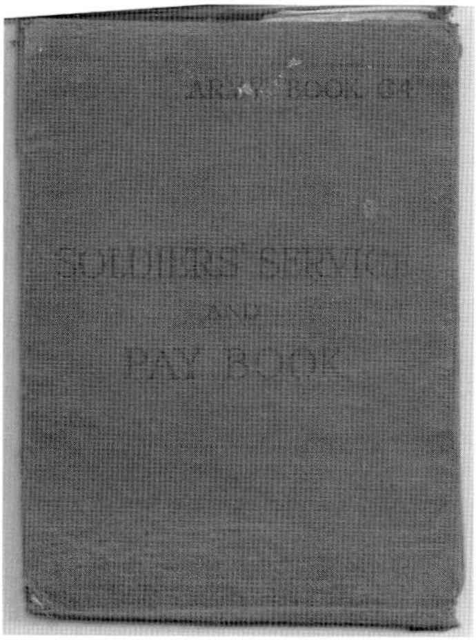

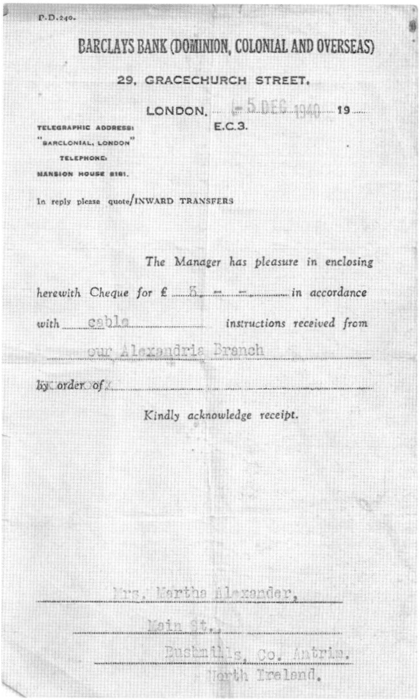

P.D.240.

BARCLAYS BANK (DOMINION, COLONIAL AND OVERSEAS)

29, GRACECHURCH STREET.

LONDON, 5 DEC 1940 19

E.C.3.

TELEGRAPHIC ADDRESS: "BARCLONIAL, LONDON"
TELEPHONE: MANSION HOUSE 8181.

In reply please quote/INWARD TRANSFERS

The Manager has pleasure in enclosing herewith Cheque for £ 5 – – *in accordance with* cable *instructions received from* our Alexandria Branch *by order of*

Kindly acknowledge receipt.

Mrs. Martha Alexander,
Main St.,
Bushmills, Co. Antrim,
North Ireland.

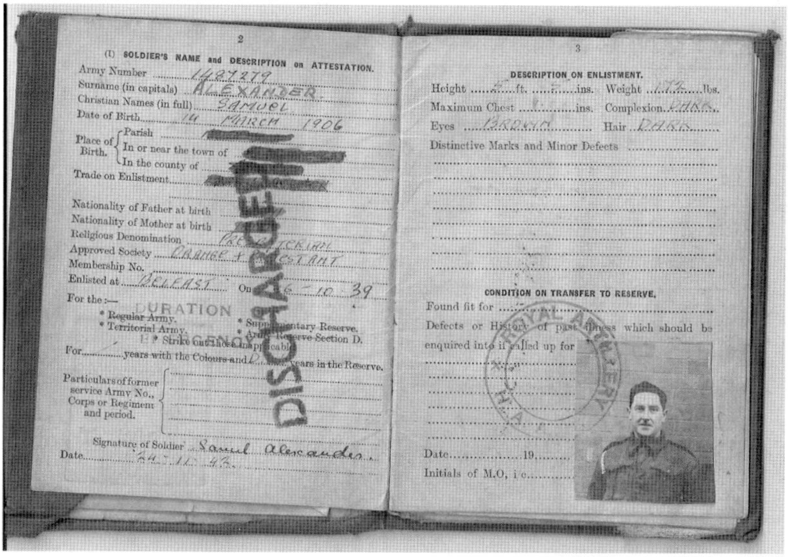

2

(1) SOLDIER'S NAME and DESCRIPTION on ATTESTATION.

Army Number 1487279
Surname (in capitals) ALEXANDER
Christian Names (in full) SAMUEL
Date of Birth 14 MARCH 1906
Place of Birth. Parish [redacted]
In or near the town of [redacted]
In the county of [redacted]
Trade on Enlistment [redacted]

Nationality of Father at birth
Nationality of Mother at birth
Religious Denomination PRESBYTERIAN
Approved Society ORANGE + PROTESTANT
Membership No.
Enlisted at BELFAST On 6-10-39
For the :—
* Regular Army. DURATION
* Territorial Army.
* Supplementary Reserve.
* Army Reserve Section D.
* Strike out those inapplicable.
For ...... years with the Colours and ...... years in the Reserve.
Particulars of former service Army No., Corps or Regiment and period.

Signature of Soldier Samuel Alexander
Date 24-11-43

DISCHARGED

3

DESCRIPTION ON ENLISTMENT.

Height 5 ft. 5 ins. Weight 172 lbs.
Maximum Chest ...... ins. Complexion DARK
Eyes BROWN Hair DARK
Distinctive Marks and Minor Defects

CONDITION ON TRANSFER TO RESERVE.

Found fit for
Defects or History of past illness which should be enquired into if called up for

Date ...... 19......
Initials of M.O. i/c ......

ROYAL ARTILLERY

The Commonwealth War Graves Commission

The commission was established by Royal Charter in 1917, and pays tribute to the 1,7000,000 men and women of the Commonwealth forces who died in the two

world wars. Since it started the Commission has constructed 2,500 cemeteries and plots, erecting headstones over graves and in instances where the remains are missing, inscribing the names of the dead on permanent memorials which is over 750,000.

Over I million casualties are now commemorated at military and civil sites in some 150 countries.

Stone walls and wrought-iron gates are a common feature at all the cemeteries. There are registers containing the names, some details of the serviceman and a cemetery plan with grave references.

You will find The Cross of Sacrifice in cemeteries with over 40 graves, this represents the faith of the majority. In the larger cemeteries with over a 1,000

Typical Commonwealth War Graves Cemetery

burials you will see the Stone of Remembrance to commemorate those of all faiths and those with none

Each grave is marked by uniform headstone, differentiated only by their inscriptions, the national emblem or regimental badge, rank, name, unit, date of death and age of each casualty is inscribed above an appropriate religious symbol and a more personal dedication chosen by relatives.

In countries like Burma and Thailand where there is risk of earth movement, graves are marked instead by bronze plaques on low pedestals.

More than half of the 1,700 acres under the Commission's control is given over to horticulture making maintenance a year round task. The original idea was to create an environment where visitors could experience a sense of peace in a beautiful and serene setting. Wherever possible, species native to the casualties countries were planted to enhance sentimental associations with the gardens of home.

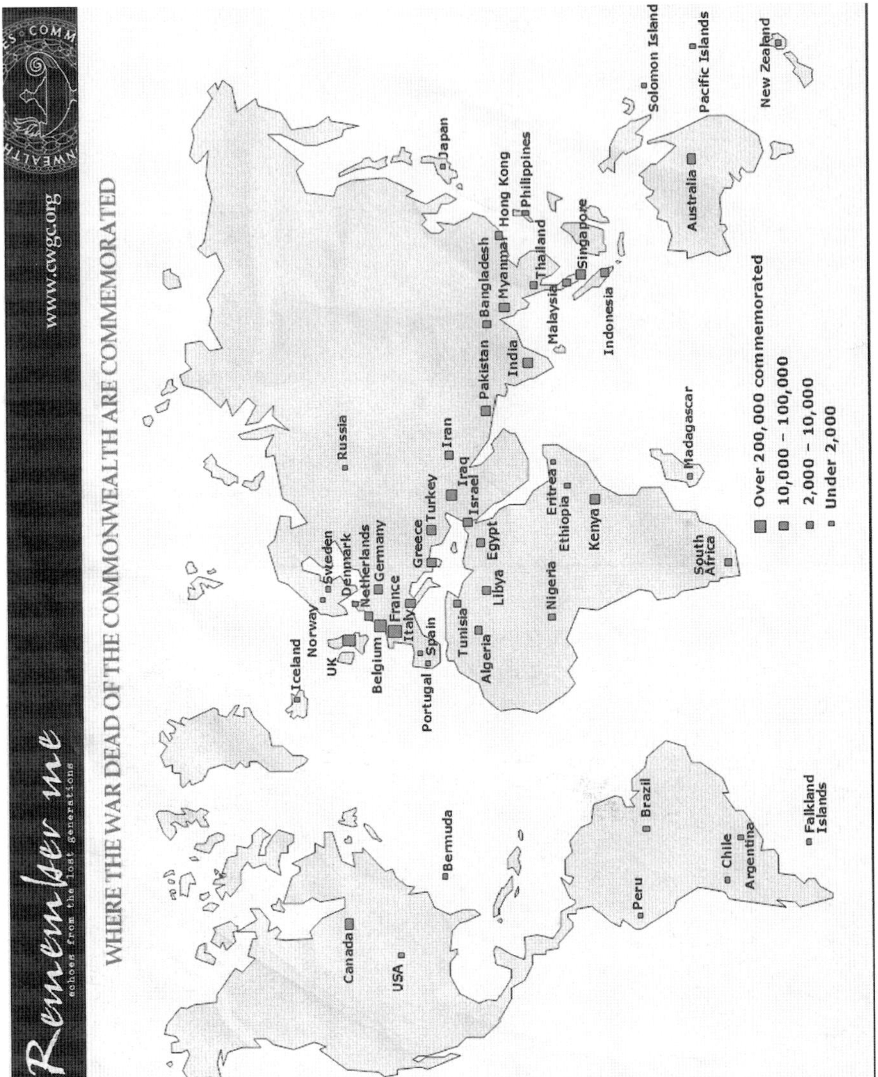
Remember me
echoes from the lost generations
www.cwgc.org
WHERE THE WAR DEAD OF THE COMMONWEALTH ARE COMMEMORATED
Canada
USA
Bermuda
Peru
Brazil
Chile
Argentina
Falkland Islands
Iceland
UK
Norway
Sweden
Denmark
Netherlands
Belgium
Germany
France
Italy
Portugal
Spain
Greece
Turkey
Russia
Algeria
Tunisia
Libya
Egypt
Israel
Iraq
Iran
Nigeria
Eritrea
Ethiopia
Kenya
South Africa
Madagascar
Pakistan
India
Bangladesh
Myanmar
Thailand
Malaysia
Singapore
Indonesia
Hong Kong
Philippines
Japan
Australia
Solomon Island
Pacific Islands
New Zealand
Over 200,000 commemorated
10,000 - 100,000
2,000 - 10,000
Under 2,000

BUSHMILLS WAR MEMORIAL

During the first two weeks of July 1953, a number of collectors have visited each home in the Bushmills area collecting donations towards the erection of a plaque on the war memorial bearing the names of those from the district who paid the supreme sacrifice in the 1939-1945 war.

Collectors reported that their task was simplified by the ready and generous response to their appeal, which resulted in the sum of £203 17s and 6d being realised.

It will be recalled that the Bushmills War Memorial was amongst the first to be erected after the 1914-1918 war and it was unveiled on 5th November, 1921 by the late The Hon. Lady Edith Macnaghten.

The memorial plaque for the Second World War was unveiled in March, 1953. The attendance of the general public and ex-servicemen was extremely large.

The British Legion from Upperlands, Garvagh, Portstewart, Portrush and Bushmills were also present. The service commenced with the singing of the 100th psalm, followed by prayer and scripture readings by Rev. S. Alexander

B.A. Dunluce Presbyterian church. Mrs A. O'B.Trail Ballylough House, Bushmills unveiled the plaque in remembrance of the twenty nine men in all branches of the services, and one woman, all from Bushmills district who made the supreme sacrifice, and of three who died later as a result of their service.

Rev. S. Eaton M.A. H.C.F. Bushmills Presbyterian Church read the names inscribed on the plaques and performed the Dedication service.

A short but impressive address was delivered by the Rector of Dunluce Parish Church, Rev. F.G. Guy M.A. H.C.F. and chairman of the Bushmills branch of the British Legion.

The solemn service concluded with the singing of 'Abide with me' followed by the National Anthem.

Chancellor F.G. Guy being presented with a Certificate to honor his role as President of B.R.B.L.
Presented by Tony Cochrane and Colin Sinclair both ex R.A.F.

DUNLUCE PARISH CHURCH

WAR MEMORIAL UNVEILED

A War Memorial tablet in Irish limestone, erected by the congregation of Dunluce Parish, Bushmills, to the memory of fourteen parishioners who gave their lives in the cause of freedom in the Second World War 1939-1945 was unveiled and dedicated at a special service.

Local ex-servicemen assembled at the British Legion clubroom and paraded to the service led by 1st Dunluce boys Brigade band. A halt was made at Market Square opposite the town war memorial where the band played "The Flowers of the Forest".

The church service was conducted by Rev. F.G. Guy M.A. H.C.F and C.F. Lieut-Colonel A. O'B. Trail O.B.E. D.L. J.P. President of the Bushmills branch of the British Legion who read the lesson. The memorial tablet was unveiled and dedicated.

The Act of Remberance was given by Rev. Guy and was followed by the Last Post and Reveille. The hymn "The Supreme Sacrifice" was sang by the choir with Miss E. Davidson at the organ.

The sermon was preached by the Rev. J. P. Stevenson who took as his text "My Table Thou has Furnished". He referred to the memorial tablet, and said that while it would furnish the church and be a visible token of thankfulness to those who had given their lives in the cause of freedom, this in itself was not enough, thankfulness should be accompanied by dedication.

March 18th 1950

BALLINTOY PARISH CHURCH

Ballintoy Parish has two War memorials, one to the Great War and the other to the Second World War.

The Memorial of white marble on a dark background bears the names of those from the Parish who served and those who died in the 1939-1945 War.

Fus. W.H. Mitchell does not appear on the Bushmills War Memorial. William Henry Mitchell was in the Royal Irish Fusiliers and was killed in Hafia, on 28th November, 1938 when his battalion was engaging a party of armed bandits.

His father received the Palestine Medal posthumously on behalf of his son.

Ever remembered by his father, sisters and brothers, Mary, Katie, Archie and Charlie of Craigalappin also sister Lizzie and brother-in-law Alex Shirley of Toberkeigh.

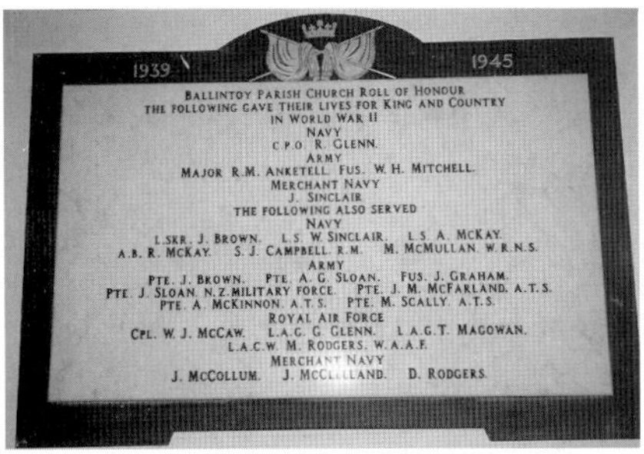

Major R. M. Anketell is commemorated on Ballycastle War Memorial. He was with the East African Artillery and died on active service while stationed in the Seychelles. He is buried in Victoria Cemetery.

THEY GAVE THEIR LIVES FOR THEIR COUNTRY

NAVY: CPO ROBERT GLENN

ARMY: MAJOR R.M. ANKETELL, FUS. W.H. MITCHELL

MERCHANT NAVY: J. SINCLAIR

DUNLUCE PRESBYTERIAN CHURCH

WAR MEMORIAL DEDICATED

A beautiful teak table for use in the porch of the church was un veiled and Dedicated as a 1939-1945 war memorial at a service in Dunluce Presbyterian.

The table, a gift from the congregation, is inscribed with the names of twenty members who served in various branches of the forces, two of whom;

SERG. GUNNER JAMES MACREADY ROYAL AIR FORCE

SERG. GUNNER WILLIAM RANKIN ROYAL AIR FORCE

LOST THEIR LIVES WHEN ON OPERATIONAL FLIGHTS AGAINST THE ENEMY.

To the Glory of God and in Loving Memory

The address was given by Rev. Samuel Eaton M.A. Bushmills, an ex-R.A.F. Chaplin. The unveiling ceremony was performed by Mrs. Hugh Torrens, sister of the late Serg. James Macready and Ian Ranken, a younger brother of the late Serg. William Ranken.

The dedication was by the Rev. Mr Eaton and Rev. Mr Alexander offered the dedicatory prayer, which was followed by the sounding of the last post and reveille by Mr D. Graham of Portrush.

In attendance was members of the British Legion, Dunluce Companys of the Boys Brigade and 1st Bushmills pipe band. Major H.F. Whitburn, vice chairman of the Legion was in charge of the parade.

Sunday May, 26th 1951

BUSHMILLS PRESBYTERIAN CHURCH

DEDICATION OF WAR MEMORIAL

A special service was held on the afternoon of Sunday 18th May 1952 at which a Memorial tablet inscribed with the names of members of the congregation, who served in the different branches of H.M. Forces during the Second World War, was unveiled and dedicated.

There was an impressive parade of ex-servicemen and women who represented Bushmills, Dervock and Ballymoney.

1st Dunluce Company B.B. pipe band led the British Legions, Girl Guides and Boys Brigade to Bushmills Presbyterian Church, past the war memorial to the church. Mr. James Cochrane, under the command of Mr. W.R. Knox M.B.E. of Portrush led the parade.

The service was conducted by Rev. Samuel Eaton, M.A. H.C.F. During the singing of the 100th Psalm, the Standards of each branch of the British Legion and of the youth organisations were received by the Reverend Eaton and the Reverend F.G.Guy M.A. H.C.F. from Dunluce Parish Church, who read the scripture lesson.

The brass tablet, which is an extension of the memorial tablet of the Great War erected in the porch of the church, had a beautiful oak surround added.

It is inscribed with forty-two names, including those of:

SERGEANT AIR GUNNER JAMES ELLIOTT ROYAL AIR FORCE.
LANCE-CORPORAL FRED WILKINSON ROYAL INNISKILLING FUSILIERS.
PRIVATE JOSEPH WATTERS ROYAL ULSTER RIFLES.

THEY MADE THE SUPREME SACRIFICE

The unveiling ceremony was by Mr. John Elliott sen. Of Turfahun, four of whose family served in the forces, and whose two sons were amongst those who gave their lives.

The list of names and the Exhortation was read by Rev. S. Eaton and the tablet was dedicated by the Very Reverend Dr. Erskine. A period of silence, in remembrance was followed by the sounding of the last post by, D.Graham of Portrush.

The Standard bearers received their Standards during the singing of hymn "Oh God our help in ages past" and remained in the body of the church for the singing of the National Anthem, for which the Colours were dipped in salute.

BILLY PARISH CHURCH

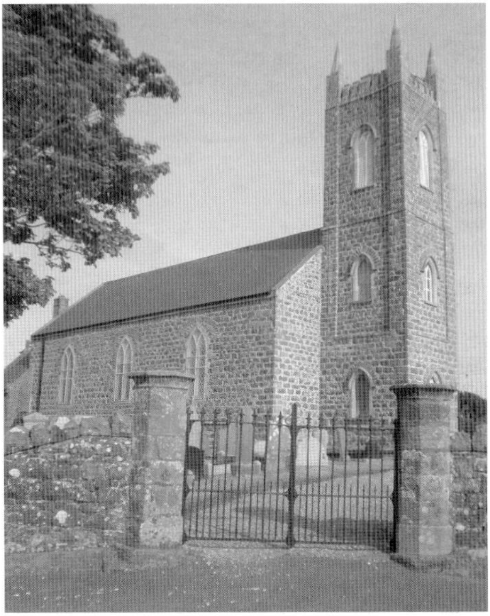

Billy Parish Church has two memorials, one to members of the parish who died in the Great War and one to the men of the Second World War.

1939-1945

THOMAS JOHN HANNA

WILLIAM KERR

JOHN McCAUHEY

DOUGLAS MCLEARON

LEST WE FORGET

The Second World War plaque was unveiled by Thomas Hanna's nephew, Jim Mathews, secton of the Church at present.

William Kerr is also remembered on Dunseverick Memorial.

Douglas McLearnon's name appears on the Memorial, but I have not traced him yet.

DUNSEVERICK PARISH CHURCH

Dunseverick Parish Church, overlooking Rathlin Island and Knocklayde, has a beautiful brass plaque engraved with the names of men who died in both World Wars.

SECOND WORLD WAR

THESE GAVE THEIR LIVES

WILLIAM SMITH
ROYAL NAVY

WILLIAM KERR
ARMY

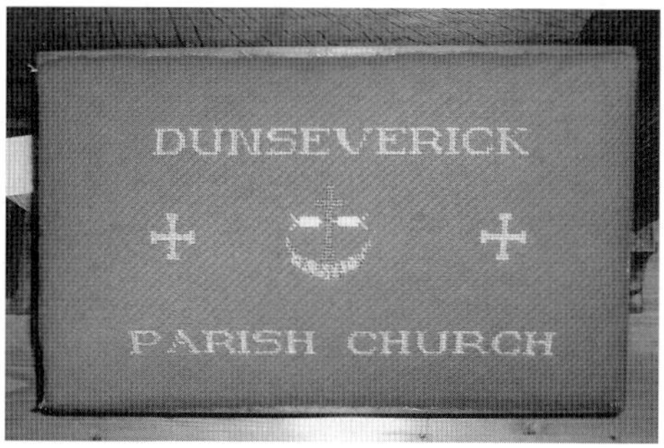

TOBERKEIGH PRESBYTERIAN CHURCH

Toberkeigh has two large brass plaques in the front porch as you enter the church. Those killed in action and those which served in the Great War are commemorated on the left.

To the right are men from the church who served or were killed in action in the Second World War.

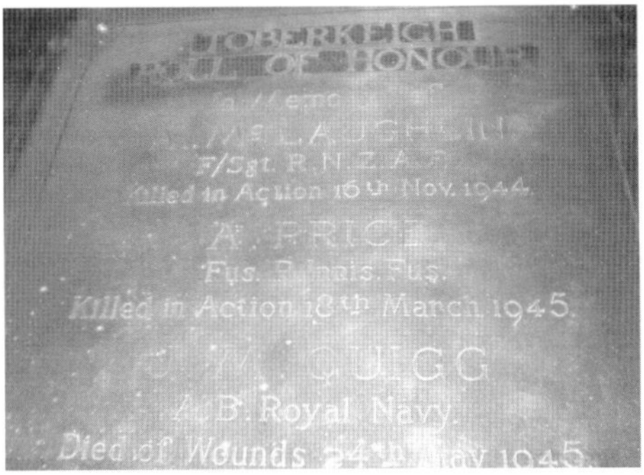

A. McLAUGHLIN
F/Sgt R.N.Z.A.F.

Killed in Action 16th November, 1944
Interred in Mosside Presbyterian Churchyard.

A. PRICE FUSILIER, ROYAL INNISKILLING FUSILIERS

Killed in Action 18th March, 1945
Buried in Faenza Cemetery, Italy.

Alexander Price was from Ballinlea and was killed in action in Italy. Aged 21 years, He had seen considerable active service and was drafted to the Mediterranean Theatre, where

He went through the greater part of the North African Campaign. He also took part in the invasion of Scilly and in the Italian battles.

Under-age but of a sturdy build "Young Sandy", as he was affectionately known to a large circle of friends, enlisted shortly after the outbreak of war.

J. M. QUIGG ABLE BODIED ROYAL NAVY
Died of wounds
24th May, 1945
Interred in Toberkeigh Presbyterian Churchyard

BUSHMILLS 1940

POST OFFICE
Postmaster G.F. Trotter
Assistant Miss M. Watters

BUSHMILLS P.E. SCHOOL
Principal John Lowry
A.Kilpatrick
Mrs Sinclair
Mrs Kilpatrick
Miss M. Kilpatrick
Mrs King

SECONDARY SCHOOL
R.C. Salisury, B.A.
H.R. Miley, B.A.
Miss Johnston B.Sc.
Miss Brown B.A.
Secretary R. Judge Portballintrae
Caretaker John Kane.

BELFAST BANK
Manager W. Mathers
Cashier J. Mc Ewen

CLERK OF PETTY SESSIONS
T.B. Gillis

REGISTRAR OF BIRTHS AND DEATHS
Dr Huey.

R.U.C. SERGEANT
W.W. McKibbin and four men

NURSES
Maternity Miss K. Cahey
District Miss Carson

MASONIC HALL
One Lodge meets first Friday of each month and One Royal Arch Chapter, Quarterly.

ORANGE HALL
W.M. Thomas Verner Lodge 914
W.M Edward Kennedy Lodge 1142
W.M Arthur McIlroy 1987
Caretaker John McKeague
William Johnston Memorial
R.B.P. No. 559
Meets second Wednesday of each month.
R.W.M. W. Esdale
Registrar Edward Kennedy

DISTRICT LODGE 21
D.M. James Wilkinson
Secretary James Torrens
Woman's L.O.L. 104
W.M. Mrs Meta Kane
D.M. Mrs Pollock

FIRST BUSHMILLS BOY SCOUTS
Rev. W.J.N. Mackey B.A.
Scouts Master

WORKING MEN'S CLUB AND BILLIARD ROOM AND LIBRARY
Caretaker Edward Kennedy

LOCAL SOLDIER AWARDED B.E.M.

Company Sergeant-Major Samuel M'Elnay, Light Anti-Aircraft Battery, R.A., has been awarded the British Empire Medal. Aged 22 years, he is the fourth son of Mr. and Mrs. James M'Elnay, Glentask, Bushmills. Shortly after the outbreak of war, he volunteered for service in H.M. Forces, and was accepted. The award was for gallantry and devotion to duty. His brother, Petty Officer Jim M'Elnay, has been in the Royal Navy for nine years, and has been mentioned in despatches on two occasions.

CHURCHES
Dunluce Parish
Rev R.H. Kimber M.A.
Caretaker Wm. Boyle
Bushmills Presbyterian
Rev. D. Maybin B.A.
Caretaker James Watters
Dunluce Presbyterian
Rev. S. Alexander B.A.
Caretaker D. Montgomery
Methodist
Rev. Thomas Steen
Caretaker William Morton
Roman Catholic
Rev. Gillen P.P.

Caretaker Mrs D. Morton.

Y.W.C.A.
Tennis Club Mrs J. Mcneill
Badminton Club A.Mccurdy

BRITISH LEGION
President Lt. Col. W. Trail D.S.O.
Chairman Alexander Mckay
Treasurer Thomas Mcfall
Secretary William Esdale

NATIONAL HEALTH INSURANCE
Orange and Protestant,
Mr William Boyle,
Presbyterian Mr G. Mcmullan
Portballintrae

MARKETS WEIGHMASTER,
PRODUCE AND CATTLE
W.Clarke, Cattle Fair 15th of
every month
Hiring Fair 15th May and 15th
November

Business Half Holiday, Thursday
"Constitution" Correspondent- James
Torrens.

COLERAINE CHRONICLE. SATURDAY, AUGUST 30, 1947.

BUSHMILLS "TOP TEN."

Bushmills "Top Ten" chosen at a dance in Bushmills Orange Hall on Friday last. Names (left to right) are:—Miss Hannah M'Alister (25), Miss Jean M'Keague (19), Miss May Glass (22), Miss Isa Carson (No. 3) (20), Miss Moira Kennedy (No. 1) (20), Mrs. Ann Purcell (No. 2) (27), Miss Mattie Alexander (16), Miss Lily Maxwell (20), Miss Florence M'Allister (20), Mrs. Martie Adamson (24).

[Photograph by Stanley Swallow, Coleraine.

WHIST DRIVE.

The prize-winners at Tuesday night's whist drive in Bushmills Men's Clubroom were A. Mogey (top score), Wm. M'Aleese and Miss B. O'Hagan. Ten tables were occupied.

HOME GUARD SERVICE.

Detachments of Ballintoy "B" Special Constabulary and Home Guard, under S.D.C. James Matthews, held a parade service to Toberkeigh Presbyterian Church on Sunday. The service was conducted by Captain Rev. V. T. Quinn, M.A., C.F., who preached an impressive sermon. Afterwards, he took the salute as the Company marched past. The offering was on behalf of the local Comforts Fund.

WAR FILMS.

A series of short films were shown by an Army film unit to members of the Bushmills platoons of Ulster Home Guard, "B" Specials and A.T.C. (Bushmills) in Dunluce Presbyterian Church Hall on Friday evening. The films depicted the war effort in Canadian factories, the fighting in Malta, and the siege of Tobruk. The show was a most interesting one.

AID TO RUSSIA.

Two little girls, Kathleen Bustard and Margaret M'Kee, of Main Street, Bushmills, have sent to Mrs. Churchill the sum of £1 1s for her Aid-to-Russia Fund. This was raised by making wool buttonholes during school holidays in October. Mrs. Churchill has written both children thanking them for the gift.

CANADIANS WELCOMED.

The people of Bushmills have been delighted to welcome three young men of the Canadian Forces on leave from England

WAR ROMANCE.

About two months ago, Mrs. Mary P. Rocco, second daughter of Mr. and Mrs. John Magowan, Upper Main St., Bushmills, sailed with her two children to U.S.A. to join her husband, who was a member of the U.S. Forces once stationed in Northern Ireland. The following extract is taken from an American newspaper: "Carmen J. Rocco saw for the first time his year-old son, Peter Carmen, when his Irish wife, formerly Mary Patricia Magowan, of Bushmills, Northern Ireland, arrived in U.S.A. Mrs. Rocco also brought with her their daughter, Mary Frances, aged two and a half. Rocco and his family are now at the home of his parents, Mr. and Mrs. Peter Rocco, 811 Reno Street, Niles, Ohio. Rocco, who met his wife while stationed with the U.S. Army in England, where she was a member of W.A.A.F., came home sixteen months ago. Since that time he has been trying to bring his family to U.S.A. Young Peter Carmen arrived in Niles in time to celebrate his first birthday, which took place on 26th March. Members of the Rocco family met at the Peter Rocco home to celebrate the event."

James Sloan

Private

Died 29th November 1942

KILLED IN ACTION.

It has been intimated to Mrs. Mary Sloan, Prolisk, Bushmills, that her son, Private James Sloan was killed in action in the Middle East on 29th November. Private Sloan emigrated to New Zealand 18 years ago, and was aged 36. He joined the New Zealand Forces at the outbreak of war and served in Greece and Crete. He was the son of the late Mr. Jackson Sloan, Prolisk, and leaves his mother and eight other members of the family to mourn his loss.

Halfaya Sollum Cemetery

To be continued . . .